Grammar and punctuation

AGES 7–8

TERM-BY-TERM PHOTOCOPIABLES

AUTHOR HUW THOMAS

With thanks to the children of Springfield School, Sheffield

EDITOR STEVEN CARRUTHERS

ASSISTANT EDITOR ROANNE DAVIS

SERIES DESIGNER CLAIRE BELCHER

DESIGNERS RACHAEL HAMMOND

AND LYNDA MURRAY

ILLUSTRATIONS JANE COPE

Designed using Adobe Pagemaker

Published by Scholastic Ltd, Villiers House, Clarendon Avenue, Leamington Spa, Warwickshire CV32 5PR
Text © Huw Thomas

© 1999 Scholastic Ltd

7 8 9 0   5 6

British Library Cataloguing-in-Publication Data
A catalogue record for this book is available from the British Library.

ISBN 0-590-63649-9

Acknowledgements
The publishers gratefully acknowledge permission to reproduce the following copyright material:
The Agency for the use of 'Our car' by Tony Bradman from *Things That Go* compiled by Tony Bradman ©1989, Tony Bradman (1989, Blackie). All rights reserved and enquiries to The Agency (London) Ltd, 24 Pottery Lane, London W11 4LZ.
Andersen Press for the use of text from *Way Home* by Libby Hathorn © 1994, Libby Hathorn (Published in Great Britain by Andersen Press Ltd, London; 1994, first published by Random House Australia).
Gerald Duckworth & Co. Ltd for 'Overheard on a salt marsh' by Harold Munro from *The Collected Poems of Harold Munro* © 1933, Harold Munro (1933, Gerald Duckworth & Co Ltd).
The Literary Trustees of Walter de la Mare and the Society of Authors as their representatives for the use of 'The Listeners' by Walter de la Mare from *The Complete Poems of Walter de la Mare* (1969) (USA: 1970).
Penguin Books Australia for the use of an extract from *Spaghetti Pig Out* by Paul Jennings © 1988, Paul Jennings (1989, Puffin).
Penguin Books Ltd for the use of an extract from *Something Else* by Kathryn Cave © 1994, Kathryn Cave (1994, Viking).
Walker Books for extracts from *Farmer Duck* by Martin Waddell and Helen Oxenbury Text © 1991, Martin Waddell (1991, Walker Books Ltd.); extract from *Where's My Teddy?* by Jez Alborough © 1992, Jez Alborough (1992, Walker Books); extract from *Owl Babies* by Martin Waddell © 1992, Martin Waddell (1992, Walker Books) and an extract from *Granny* by Anthony Horowitz © 1995, Anthony Horowitz (1995, Walker).

Every effort has been made to trace copyright holders for the works reproduced in this book, and the publishers apologize for any inadvertent omissions.

Contents

Introduction

Welcome to grammar and punctuation

'As a writer I know that I must select studiously the nouns, pronouns, verbs, adverbs, etcetera, and by a careful syntactical arrangement make readers laugh, reflect or riot.'

Maya Angelou

The *Scholastic Literacy Skills: Grammar and punctuation* series equips teachers with resources and subject training enabling them to teach grammar and punctuation at Key Stage 2. The focus of the resource is on what is sometimes called *sentence-level* work, so called because grammar and punctuation primarily involve the construction and understanding of sentences.

Many teachers approach the teaching of grammar bringing with them a lot of past memories. Some will remember school grammar lessons as the driest of subjects, involving drills and parsing, and will wonder how they can make it exciting for their own class. At the other end of the spectrum, some will have received relatively little formal teaching of grammar at school. Recent research by the Qualifications and Curriculum Authority found a lack of confidence among Key Stage 2 teachers when it came to teaching sentence structure, commenting that:

'Where teachers were less confident, it tended to be because sentence structure had not formed part of their own education.'

(QCA, 1998, page 28)

In other words there are teachers who, when asked to teach clause structure or prepositions, feel at a bit of a loss. They are being asked to teach things they are not confident with themselves. Even worse, they think they should be confident in these things.

Grammar can evoke lethargy, fear, irritation, pedantry and despondency. Yet at the beginning of this introduction we have one of the greatest modern writers presenting her crafting of sentences as an exciting and tactical process that has a powerful effect on her readers. Can this be the grammar that makes teachers squirm or run?

The *Scholastic Literacy Skills: Grammar and punctuation* series

The *Scholastic Literacy Skills: Grammar and punctuation* series works from the premise that grammar and punctuation can be interesting and dynamic – but on one condition. The condition is that the teaching of these aspects of grammar must be related to *real texts* and *practical activities* that experiment with language, investigate the use of language in real contexts and find the ways in which grammar and punctuation are used in our day-to-day talk, writing and reading. The series is based upon five principles about the teaching of grammar:

1. Meaningful sentence-level work
In looking at how sentences are put together in a text, an appreciation of the function of that text is crucial. As children investigate the structure of sentences or the types of words they contain, they need to be aware of them as communicative acts; the purposes of the various pieces of writing considered in this resource play a crucial role in the activities. As children work through various aspects of *Grammar and punctuation*, teachers should reflect on how individual children are using their developing understanding of sentences in the rest of their written and spoken work.

2. Language from real life
As far as is possible, children need to work with language set in real-life contexts rather than always looking at contrived texts and exercises. Instead of made-up newspapers, for example, they need to look at extracts from the real thing. They need the encouragement to look at language in their environment, the books they enjoy and the things they and their peers say to one another. These are some of the most valuable resources available for language work because in using them children will apply what they learn to texts they know.

The *Scholastic Literacy Skills: Grammar and punctuation* series does contain a number of exercises in which sentences have been constructed purely to provide examples of the use of a particular type of word or punctuation mark. However, this is always complemented by more realistic uses of language. The aim is consistently to refer children to genuine texts extracted from real books and actual newspapers. For this reason the *Scholastic Literacy Skills: Grammar and punctuation* series asks children to work on grammar and punctuation using texts as diverse as fables, jokes, book blurbs, leaflets, children's own writing, comic stories, poems, scripts, comedy sketches, labels, classic poetry, texts in various dialects… in fact the mix is as rich and lively as the children's own language experiences should be. A flick through the photocopiable material in this book will show the commitment of the series to varied and interesting texts based on the conviction that relevant and appropriate texts will motivate children to learn about language.

3. Teachers as active participants

The 'rules' of grammar and punctuation are not static aspects of language; we are all continually revising and developing them. The most competent and experienced of writers can still find new and interesting features of these aspects of language and develop their own use of English. Because of this the *Scholastic Literacy Skills: Grammar and punctuation* series equips the teacher with subject knowledge, definitions and explanations as

preparation for the subject matter of each unit. It is important that, as far as is possible, teachers join in with activities. If, for example, an activity involves bringing a leaflet in from home and looking at the use of persuasive language, then everyone should take part. What many teachers have found is that grammar and punctuation can be great levellers. In other words, as children investigate these aspects of language, the teacher can join in and genuinely participate in developing his or her own use of English.

4. Structure is essential

While the *Scholastic Literacy Skills: Grammar and punctuation* series is full of interesting and lively material, it is underpinned by a clear and deliberate structure. The sentence-level aspects of English are so many and so varied that teaching them effectively demands a structured approach. The basic aim has been to provide a clearly structured resource that uses common sense and introduces features such as sentence structure and punctuation in ways that build continuity and progression into children's learning.

The half-term sections and units of each book are structured in a way that develops the teaching of grammar and punctuation in Key Stage 2 in England, Wales and Northern Ireland, and Levels C–E in Scotland. Care has been taken to encompass the National Literacy Strategy *Framework for Teaching* (DfEE, 1998), so that teachers following the strategy can use these books with the confidence that they are delivering all the appropriate sentence-level objectives for each year group.

5. Active enjoyment

This is not a book of basic drills. The *Scholastic Literacy Skills: Grammar and punctuation* series was put together in the knowledge that grammar and punctuation *can* be taught in a dry and dull way but with a commitment to do the complete opposite. With this in mind, the activities are constructed in a way that involves a lot of active investigative work and play with language.

The books provide a balanced 'diet' of exercises mixed with practical, hands-on activities, including researching language, recording and analysing speech, drama activities, games and advertising. The underlying premise is that language is interesting, that understanding it can be fascinating and that working with it can be fun.

Grammar and punctuation: do they matter?

Any introduction to the teaching of grammar and punctuation sets up a stall in the middle of one of the hottest debates in the teaching of English. For this reason it is necessary to say a few things about the usefulness and purpose of sentence-level teaching.

Background

There was a period from the 1960s to the 1980s when the teaching of grammar in particular and punctuation to a lesser extent was not in vogue. This was, in part, due to research projects in the 1960s that claimed to have shown the teaching of such aspects of English to be 'useless' and even 'harmful' (for example, Harris's research summarized in QCA, 1998). The Kingman Report in 1988 marked a change in this situation. After a period in which grammar had lain dormant, this report promoted the use of grammatical terminology in relevant contexts and recommended that all trainee teachers receive a large amount of 'direct tuition of knowledge about language' (HMSO, 1988, page 69).

A large portion of the Kingman Report was devoted to considering the talk and work of children. These were examined and the implicit linguistic knowledge in these activities was drawn out, such as the six-year-old whose writing demonstrated implicit understanding of subordinate clauses and qualifying phrases (HMSO, 1988, page 36). Taking the example of discussion about pronouns they made a comment that:

'Since… teacher and pupil need, in discussion, a word which refers to a class of terms (i.e. pronouns) there is no good reason not to use that term.'

(HMSO, 1988, page 13)

What Kingman raised was the usefulness of knowledge about language in the teaching of English.

Reasons for teaching grammar and punctuation

Grammar and punctuation are sometimes seen as symbols of a golden age when children were taught 'the basics'. This sort of talk has not served the subject well. It took some time for the Kingman recommendations to permeate into the English curriculum in a thorough and progressive way. It is crucial that, as teachers embark on the teaching of grammar and punctuation, they do so with a clear sense of exactly what it is these subjects will provide the learner with. The *Scholastic Literacy Skills: Grammar and punctuation* series is based on the following theoretical understanding of the value of teaching grammar and punctuation.

❑ Understanding and using terminology used to describe aspects of grammar and punctuation equips children with the vocabulary they need to discuss language. For example, it can be much easier to discuss the ambiguities that can surround the use of pronouns with children if they understand the term 'pronoun' and are beginning to use it to describe some of the words they use.

❑ Looking at aspects of sentence construction stimulates children to reflect on their own use of language. For example, many teachers try to discourage the overuse of the word 'and…' as in 'I went out and I saw my friend and we played in the park and we went to the shop and we bought…' and so on. Guiding children out of this overuse of 'and' is a task with which many teachers are familiar. It can be greatly enhanced by an understanding of certain aspects of grammar and punctuation such as how sentences break up a piece of writing so that it makes sense; other words and terms that can connect sentences and clauses together; ways in which sentences and clauses can be punctuated; and the functions performed by specific connecting words and phrases.

❑ There are links within the subject of English that make one aspect vital to the understanding of another. For example, the understanding of how certain texts address and persuade their readers involves an awareness of the concept of 'person' in pronouns and verbs. Another example is the way in which the use of the comma can depend on an understanding of how clauses function. Many aspects of grammar and punctuation play vital roles in other areas of English.

❑ Grammar and punctuation can provide a means of evaluating how effectively and clearly a spoken or written piece of language communicates. For example, the teacher who is exasperated by a child's constant use of the word 'nice' to describe everything he or she likes might find some work on adjectives steers the child towards new ways of describing.

❑ An appreciation of grammar and punctuation empowers children to make full use of the English language. Starting with simple sentences, children can move on to an understanding of features such as nouns, verbs, commas, clauses, adjectives and adverbs. Grammar and punctuation become the tools that enable children to explore new ways of expressing themselves in their writing.

Introduction

❏ Linguistics, the study of language, is a subject in its own right. Looking at grammar and punctuation gives children their first encounters with this fascinating subject. The discussion of language features such as dialect words and expressions introduces children to the subject of sociolinguistics. This is the study of how language functions within society and it is just one example of the way in which the study of language can be an interesting subject in itself.

Working with *Scholastic Literacy Skills: Grammar and punctuation*

Unit structure

Each book in the *Scholastic Literacy Skills: Grammar and punctuation* series is broken up into six sections, each of which is structured to provide resources for a half-term. Within each section, material is gathered together to give a specific content to that half-term, indicated on the contents page. Each section contains two 'posters' that present some of the material covered over the half-term in an accessible form for reference. These are so named because it is recommended that they are enlarged to A3 size (or A2, using two A3 sheets) and placed on display while the units are undertaken. They can also be used as shared texts in reading activities as well as posters provided for reference in the classroom.

Each half-term section is split into five units, each dealing with a specific aspect of grammar or punctuation. Within each unit there are three photocopiables. These are prefaced by introductory material, structured under the following headings:

Objective: the learning objective(s) for the unit.

Language issues: explanatory material on the issues covered in the unit. These are predominantly focused on the subject matter of the unit and can provide clarification for the teacher, equipping him or her towards delivery of the unit.

Ways of teaching: notes on the teaching of the subject matter. This section can provide specific points about the approach to be adopted and the terminology to be used, and has a specific bearing upon the teaching of the unit.

About the activities: a note that clarifies any information the teacher may need for the unit. In some cases this is a full explanation of the activity; in others it is just a hint on the presentation of the subject matter.

Following up: optional activity suggestions to follow up the content of the unit. These can be specific activities but they can also be notes as to how the content of the unit can dovetail with other aspects of English.

Differentiation

The activities in each book are produced with the average ability of the relevant year group in mind. They draw upon the work of the National Literacy Project, a pilot project that led to the production of the National Literacy Strategy (DfEE, 1998). Differentiation should be possible within each unit in the following ways:

❏ *Providing support* in the way activities are staged. When, for example, there are three stages to an activity, the teacher can assist children who need support through one or more of the stages.

❏ *Reducing the amount of material.* If an activity asks children to complete a certain number of tasks, such as the ordering of ten mixed-up sentences, the teacher may reduce the number for a child needing such support.

❏ *Pre-selecting appropriate material* for investigative tasks. Many of the units ask children to find texts or try activities with sentences they find in the classroom. In such cases the teacher could direct children who would find this difficult to specified sentences or previously selected material.

❏ *Providing follow-up work.* More able children can benefit from being given one of the tasks under the heading 'Following up', extending their work based on the objective of the unit.

A 'resource', not a 'scheme'

The photocopiables in each book are a support for teaching. While they may carry notes to inform children, the actual teaching of the learning objective can only be achieved through discussion of the language issues supported by the use of the photocopiable sections. This takes us back to the idea of the teacher as an active participant. These materials are to be used by the class working in conjunction with the teacher and should support the teacher's explanation and discussion of the subject matter in each unit.

It should be stressed that *Scholastic Literacy Skills: Grammar and punctuation* does not intend to provide a scheme that children slavishly work their way through. It is a flexible teaching resource. While each book provides the subject matter appropriate to the age group at which it is aimed, the teacher will soon realize there is more material in each book than a class could be expected to cover in one year. The introductory pages at the start of each half-termly section and the language issues sections are there to enable teachers to select the photocopiable page, poster, or activity from the 'Following up' section, that best supports their own planning, the needs of the class – and personal preferences.

Texts, texts and more texts!
Various activities call for a range of resources. Check each activity to see what is needed in the way of paper, scissors, glue and so on. The most valuable resource, however, is a rich variety of texts available for the children's use – collect together a truly mixed bag of old and new texts (familiar and unfamiliar), including leaflets, menus, newspapers, comics, letters, junk mail, posters… the broader the range the better!

Introduction to Ages 7–8

The thirty units comprising *Scholastic Literacy Skills: Grammar and Punctuation, Ages 7–8* have as their objective to provide a grounding in the basic features of sentences, grammar and punctuation.

A knowledge of sentences, grammar and punctuation is acquired in Key Stage 1 and this will be revised and built upon in this book. This is evidenced by the revision of the use of the full stop within sentences, while the introduction of the comma builds upon the children's knowledge gained in Key Stage 1.

The constituent elements of an understanding of grammar are presented in these units and include work on verbs, adjectives and singular and plural nouns. The use of texts to develop children's understanding of each element within context is clearly emphasized. This is particularly important in ensuring that children's initial understanding of what constitutes a verb or an adjective is securely based.

Pronouns, prepositions and conjunctions are introduced enabling further understanding of sentence construction. Use of speech marks and other dialogue punctuation complete this term's work.

Verbs

Contents of Term 1a

Unit 1:
Collecting verbs
Learn the appropriate use of the term 'verb'
Learn the function of verbs in sentences, observing their key role in sentences

Unit 2:
Changing verbs
Learn the function of verbs in sentences, collecting and classifying examples and experimenting with changing them
Learn to use awareness of grammar to decipher new or unfamiliar words

Unit 3:
Comparing verbs
Experiment with changing verbs in a sentence and evaluating the result

Unit 4:
Tenses
Understand the appropriate and consistent use of verb tenses

Unit 5:
Investigating verbs
Learn to consider the functions of verbs in sentences

This half-term

This half-term will provide children with a thorough introduction to verbs. It includes activities that identify and understand the role verbs play in sentences but there is also an emphasis upon trying things out with this class of words. Verbs are essential elements within a sentence; upon them, the meaning depends. Altering the verb within a sentence can change the meaning in a major or more subtle way; both of these options are explored in these units.

The units also provide a grounding in the concept of verb tense.

Poster notes

Past, present, future
This poster provides examples of the past and present tenses and the future form of a few common verbs. It can be displayed as a reminder of how these three tenses operate. Boxes or whole columns can be covered leaving groups to suggest what the missing words could be. It illustrates important points about past and future tenses, which children soon notice when faced with the three columns.

Pin people
This collection of pin people provides a variety of actions and the verbs that denote them. It is similar to the sort of chart children are asked to construct in 'Little boxes' (Unit 1).

Past, present and future

In the past I	Now I	In the future I
walked	walk	will walk
ran	run	will run
crawled	crawl	will crawl
said	say	will say
sneezed	sneeze	will sneeze
thought	think	will think

Pin people

crawling	swinging	painting	jumping
singing	~~hopping~~	standing	eating
chopping	climbing	cycling	laughing
sitting	skipping	falling	waving
sneezing	meeting	talking	juggling
hiding	crying	skating	reading

Scholastic Literacy Skills

Collecting verbs

Objective
Learn the appropriate use of the term 'verb'
Learn the function of verbs in sentences, observing their key role in sentences

Language issues
The verb is often considered to be the most important part of a sentence. It shows the action or happening that is taking place. In this unit children are introduced to the idea in a way that will lead them to locate their own examples of verbs in a variety of texts. They will begin to encounter words that can function as a verb or as another type of word.

Auxiliary verbs
The children will also begin to look at sentences containing an auxiliary verb. These verbs (sometimes called 'helping' verbs) act as auxiliaries to other verbs. They make the main verb in a phrase conditional. In a sentence like 'I play ludo' I am describing an action I actually do. An auxiliary verb like 'can' slots into the sentence to make 'I can play ludo'. This sentence says I can play it, not that I necessarily do.

The verbs known as the primary verbs ('be', 'have', and 'do') can be main verbs – 'I am running', 'I have a cold', and 'I did nothing' or auxiliary verbs – 'I was making a cake', 'I have told you once' and 'I didn't see you'. 'Used', 'ought', 'need' and 'dare' can be used as auxiliaries or as verbs on their own ('I need a drink' and 'I need to drink a drink').

The other auxiliary verbs, are:'can', 'could', 'may', 'might', 'must', 'will', 'shall', 'would' and 'should'. They always act as auxiliaries to other verbs.

Auxilliaries can often take the 'n't' contraction to make constructions like: 'haven't', 'wasn't' and 'can't'.

Ways of teaching
The focus of this section is upon finding and identifying verbs in various contexts, whether it be rooting out ones that spring to mind when we are thinking about actions, or verbs we encounter in a range of texts.

About the activities
Photocopiable: Little boxes
One of the most accessible ways of understanding the function of verbs is for children to consider the words they use for various actions. This activity sets before them the challenge of generating as many different actions as they can. As children undertake this activity they sometimes present the same action with a different label (for example, two pictures of a runner, one labelled 'running' and the other labelled 'sprinting'). The teacher may want to introduce them to the term *synonym* (two words with similar meanings such as hit/whack, cry/weep). It can be interesting to review a class's output after this activity to see which verbs were the most common.

Photocopiable: Verb hunt
Children can encounter a range of verbs by looking at different types of text. This activity presents a range of example texts and encourages children to locate verbs. It is an activity that should naturally motivate children to point out verbs in their immediate environment, such as those to be found in displays, notices, signs, and so on.

Photocopiable: Verbs in action
As an extension to the previous activity, children can use this format to stick down and analyse material they extract from various texts in an effort to find a wide range of verbs.

As they undertake this exercise children can be shown the way in which every sentence they encounter requires a verb to make sense.

Following up
Synonyms: children can look back at the 'Little boxes' activity and consciously try presenting a set of synonymous verbs for actions such as 'crying', 'falling' and so on.

Synonyms in writing: In their story writing children can be encouraged to use synonymous verbs as a way of varying the language they use to describe actions.

Verbs in school: Children can seek out verbs in the school environment, looking at notice-boards, signs and so on.

Little boxes

❑ Try thinking of different things people do. In the boxes, draw as many different actions as you can. Write the name of the action in each box. Here are two examples.

| *running* | *skipping* |

❑ Check with a friend's little boxes. How many different verbs did you both use?

Verb Hunt

❑ Look for the verbs in these sentences. Remember that a verb can be a word or group of words. When you find a verb draw a circle round it.

❑ Collect the verbs you have found. Look at someone else's collection. Did you find the same verbs?

How many of these verbs can you use in new sentences? Turn this page over and write some sentences.

Verbs in action

❏ Look at some texts in newspapers, leaflets, old comics, packages and so on. Cut out **eight** sentences and stick them in these spaces. Write out the verbs.

INSTRUCTIONS Open the green packet and remove the nuts and bolts. Before you	Open remove

❏ Use some other texts to find more verbs.
Can you make a long list of the different verbs you find?

Changing verbs

Objective

Learn the function of verbs in sentences, collecting and classifying examples and experimenting with changing them

Learn to use awareness of grammar to decipher new or unfamiliar words

Language issues

One of the key processes in using language is selection. We select the right type of word to fit a place in a sentence. The code that guides our selection involves a number of features, including the need to make ourselves understood and the desire to choose a polite term. In this unit children look at the alternative verbs that can be used to denote a particular action or happening.

The way in which certain verbs will fit a particular context is a vital part of the reading process.

Ways of teaching

The activities in this unit focus upon the way one verb can be selected from a family of verbs to describe a particular action. Attention is drawn to the connections that link certain verbs. This principle can be explored using a range of shared texts and collating examples of verbs that children use in their own writing.

About the activities

Photocopiable: Verb links

One of the stylistic features of writing is the choice of a particular verb to cover a particular action or happening. Through learning the close links within certain families of verbs children reinforce their understanding of the type of word a verb is and build up their vocabulary.

As they undertake this activity children should be encouraged to explore the range of standard and non-standard English expressions that they use to denote a particular action.

Photocopiable: Change the verb

This activity causes children to seek out an alternative verb to cover an action. It is this sort of thesaurus-like act of selection that can enrich writing. It also reinforces the reading skill of understanding the type of word that fits a particular context. Through exchanging the verbs in the sentences in this activity children are developing their practical use of this skill.

Photocopiable: Looking at verbs in stories

By looking at the way in which writers use verbs to create an effect children should both appreciate the texts they read and build up the stock of words they can use in their own writing.

Following up

Thesauruses: Introduce children to the use of thesauruses in selecting an appropriate word for a particular action.

Definitive collections: Can the class produce the definitive list of synonymous terms to cover a particular activity like 'snitching' (telling tales)? This could involve them looking beyond the classroom to ask parents, grandparents, teachers and so on for examples from their childhood.

Redrafting: Children can apply the ideas in this section to their own writing, looking at verbs they commonly use. They can select a story they have written and consider whether they can improve the verbs they use.

Verb-pops: A list of popular verbs can be maintained in the classroom. It can be a list of ten verbs encountered in stories that grabbed the interest of the children. They can nominate and vote on candidates for the list and alter it every so often. The raised profile of certain verbs will often lead children to use items on the list in preference to words which they would have ordinarily resorted to.

Verb links

❑ Look at the four charts. At the centre there is an action or a happening. At the end of each of the five legs try to write another word for that action.

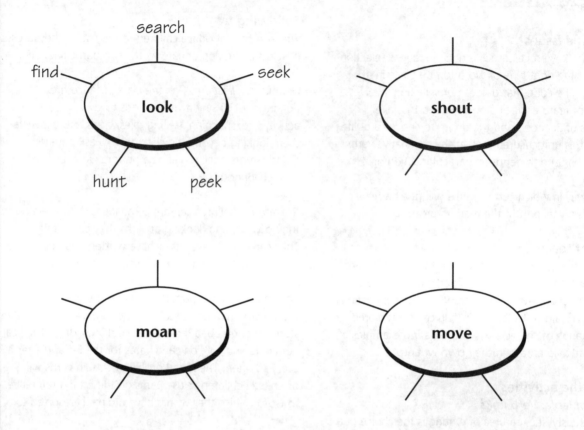

Once you have completed these you could try drawing and completing your own verb links.

Change the verb

❑ Look at the sentences below. Each of them contains a verb. Cut out the sentences and swap the verb for a juicy verb. Write your new sentence on a separate sheet of paper.

Juicy verbs

slithered	shrieked	
leaped	giggled	tumbled
dashed	halted	shattered
gobbled	bounced	pounced

Everyone laughed at the joke.

"Fire! Fire!" the boy said.

The snake went into the grass.

The window broke into many pieces.

The ball went down the stairs.

The tiger came out of the bushes.

The acrobats moved around the circus ring.

We ran for safety.

The train stopped before the broken bridge.

The greedy goblin ate all the food.

The frog went into the water.

Looking at verbs in stories

❑ Look through some story books to find different verbs. Try and find verbs that describe:
• ways of speaking (eg, whispered, shrieked)
• ways of moving (eg, ran, dived)
• ways of seeing (eg, glimpsed, spied)
• ways of having (eg, held, grabbed).

❑ Sort the verbs you find into the spaces below.

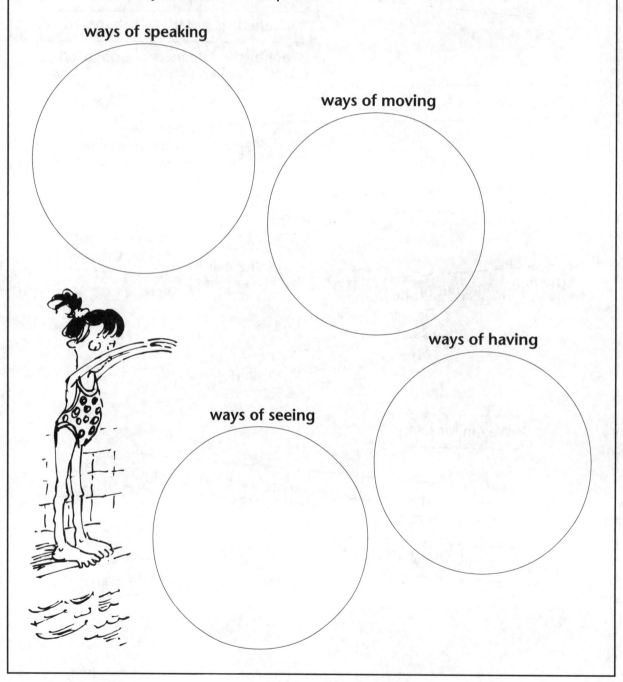

ways of speaking

ways of moving

ways of having

ways of seeing

Comparing verbs

Objective
Experiment with changing verbs in a sentence and evaluating the results

Language issues
Verbs are powerful parts of any sentence, and changing a verb makes an obvious difference to its meaning. An event can be described in a number of ways. 'He snapped the pencil', 'He broke the pencil', 'He wrecked the pencil' and 'He destroyed the pencil' all describe the same action in different ways. The selection of a particular verb can be a subtle but important part of the way in which a sentence is phrased.

Through looking at the changes in meaning that occur when substituting synonyms for verbs children can develop hands-on experience of the functional nature of language and the significance of selection of an appropriate verb for a context.

Ways of teaching
The activities presented in this unit focus upon relevant, communicative texts such as conversation and advertising. As they engage in these activities it is important that children are reminded of the audience for the sentences they are using. There will be a difference between how they describe a chocolate bar to their friends and how an advertiser describes it on television.

About the activities
Photocopiable: Our verbs
This activity revisits ground covered in Unit 2 ('Verb links'), focusing children's attention upon the verbs they actually use. The emphasis is on their actual vocabulary for the actions described. It could be an effective activity to do in pairs or groups as this will often lead children to remind each other of verbs they have not considered.

Point out to children that they can use verb phrases in which a few words denote the action (as in 'blowing a gasket').

Photocopiable: Advertising Zesto
One of the areas of language use in which words are carefully selected is advertising. In this activity children need to take on an editorial role and imagine each of the texts they consider is an idea presented to them from which they must make the best advertisement.
It is crucial that they remember their audience. They need to think of the sort of people who drink fizzy drinks and decide upon the words that would sell Zesto to them.

Once they have made their selections it can be useful to gather a class together and see which words they selected. Are the advertisements they designed similar? Are there certain points on which they all differ?

Photocopiable: Designing a Zesto advertisement
Leading on from the above activity children can use the words they found in the three examples or contributions of their own to produce an advert for Zesto. On completing the advertisement children can also design the can in which Zesto will be sold possibly using phrases from their advertising campaign.

Following up
Megalists: Make large lists of all the various terms for the actions in the 'Our verbs' exercise. Children can work in groups and see how long they can make their lists. They may want to ask other people such as parents and grandparents to contribute terms.

Contexts: Suggest a list of contexts in which language is used, such as a school letter home, chatting on the playground, speaking to grandparents, explaining something to the headteacher. Then look through the Megalist list of verbs and consider which ones would *not* be appropriate to each of those contexts. Can they explain why?

Advertising verbs: Collect advertisements from newspapers and magazines and note some of the various verbs they use. Do they use different words to describe the actions of buying and selling (do they even mention these actions – many don't!)? Children can try altering verbs in the advertisements they gather to see what effect this has upon the text.

Presenting the advertisement: Once children have devised their ideal Zesto advertisement they can present it to an audience. This could be a presentation to the rest of the class explaining why they think the language they chose will work.

Our verbs

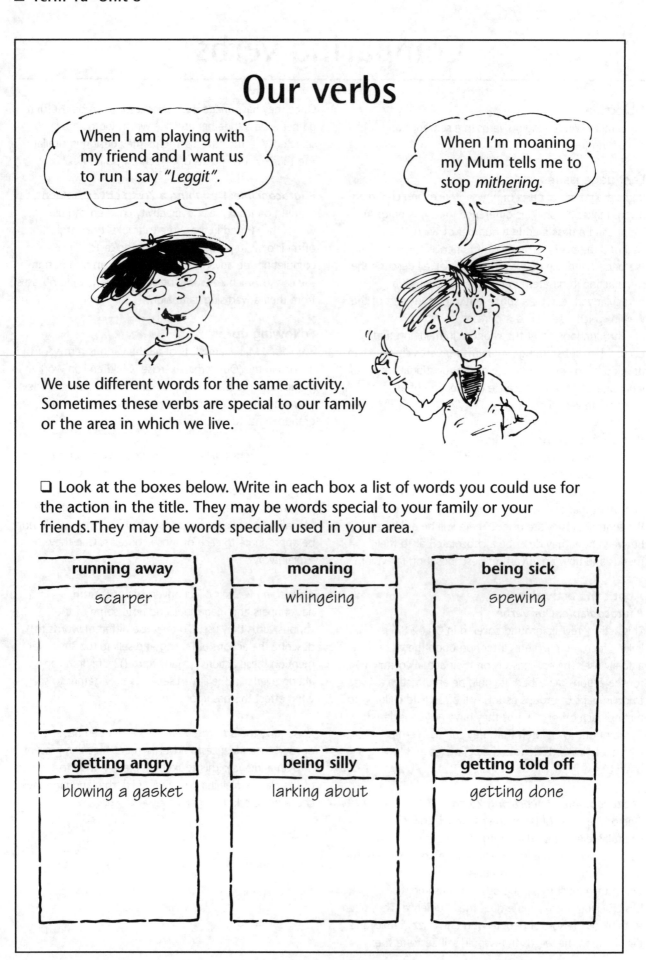

When I am playing with my friend and I want us to run I say *"Leggit"*.

When I'm moaning my Mum tells me to stop *mithering*.

We use different words for the same activity. Sometimes these verbs are special to our family or the area in which we live.

❑ Look at the boxes below. Write in each box a list of words you could use for the action in the title. They may be words special to your family or your friends.They may be words specially used in your area.

running away	moaning	being sick
scarper	whingeing	spewing

getting angry	being silly	getting told off
blowing a gasket	larking about	getting done

Advertising Zesto

❑ Look at these three versions of the same advertisement. Circle the words that are changed. Underline which word is best. Can you think of any better words to use?

I used to slouch and plod around.
My life was going nowhere.
Then I started drinking new "Zesto" filled with fizz and bursting from the bottle.
Now I leap about. I smile. I dance.
People ask "Hey! What's happened?"
I say "I'm full of zest – because I'm drinking ZESTO!"

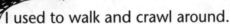

I used to walk and crawl around.
My life was turning nowhere.
Then I started buying new "Zesto" packed with fizz and fizzing from the bottle.
Now I go about. I smirk. I bop.
People say "Hey! What's changed?"
I scream "I'm full of zest – because I'm buying ZESTO!"

I used to stumble and fall around.
My life was heading nowhere.
Then I started having new "Zesto" made with fizz and shooting from the bottle.
Now I bound about. I grin. I move.
People shout "Hey! What's altered?"
I reply "I'm full of zest – because I'm guzzling ZESTO!"

Designing a Zesto advertisement

❑ Use some of the ideas you gathered from looking at the three Zesto advertisements and some of your own suggestions. Plan your own version.

I used to _____ and _____ around.

My life was _____ nowhere.

Then I started _____ new "Zesto" _____ with fizz and

_____ from the bottle.

Now I _____ about. I _____. I _____.

People _____ "Hey! What's _____?"

I _____ "I'm full of zest – because I'm _____ ZESTO!"

Tenses

Objective
Understand the appropriate and consistent use of verb tenses

Language issues
The tense is the grammatical category, expressed in forms of the verb, which locates an action in time. In English there are two simple tenses, the present tense (I walk) and the past tense (I walked). For these two tenses the verb stem itself can alter.

The future tense is made in a compound form. This means another word is added to set a verb in the future, so in the above example the simple present has the word 'will' added, creating the compound forms 'will walk'.

Ways of teaching
The first two activities in this unit involve children looking at the way the verb alters to indicate a change in tense. In the third activity this extends to consider how an action is presented as happening in the future. It will be worth clarifying the difference between the simple tenses of past and present and the compound nature of the future tense so that children are clear about the different types of change they are working with in these activities.

About the activities
Photocopiable: Verb pairs
In its straightforward form this activity involves children matching verbs of differing tenses. The activity could be extended to involve them sticking the two columns they make onto a large sheet of paper so that they can be compared side by side.

Photocopiable: Tense changer
In each of these examples children can simply change the verb to alter the tense. Some may suggest changes such as 'I was hiding' for the past tense of 'I hide' (this is, in fact the imperfect or past continuous tense). Point out that the activity can work without adding any new words, just changing the ones we have.

Bear in mind that each of the examples involves the first person singular ('I') doing the action. On completing the task children can be asked to make their own lists with new examples.

Photocopiable: Past to future
This activity introduces the compound form of the future tense. The teacher can decide whether or not to use the term 'compound' with the class. However, it is important to point out the different type of change being made here. To make the future we add another word before the verb.

Following up
Stories: Look at the different types of story telling and the uses of tense in narrative. The predominant one is the past tense. However, there are examples of stories told in the present tense. Some oral storytellers use it to create the scene before your eyes. It is also common in jokes ('This rabbit walks into a shop and buys some carrots…').

Altering tenses: Take sentences from texts such as stories and retell them in the present or in the future, looking at the alteration that is made.

Diary sentences: Ask children to offer examples of things that they do throughout the school day (such as 'We go to assembly', 'We paint a picture') and then rephrase these in the past tense, as if they were written in a diary.

Big change/Little change: Introduce children to the nature of the alteration made to verbs when they switch from present to past tense. Verbs like 'I walk' just have the '-ed' morpheme added to make 'walked'. However, some verbs (like 'I go') change completely. In the tense changer there is one verb that didn't change its appearance at all! Ask them to look for verbs that alter completely and those that just have additions to the end of the verb.

Verb pairs

❑ Cut out the verbs below. Can you find a present tense and past tense of the same verb? Place them alongside each other. Match all the present tense verbs to their past tenses.

watched	shout	stop	bit	see
wrote	find	ran	play	won
type	walked	helped	swam	stopped
run	made	win	ate	walk
shouted	help	write	saw	bite
found	eat	typed	draw	played
swim	drew	make	watch	

When you have finished you might be able to make up some pairs of your own.

Tense changer

❑ Complete this grid. Think how a present tense verb becomes past tense.

Past	Present
I found	
I lived	
	I am
	I do
	I cut
I said	
	I hide
I chased	
	I make
	I hear
I ate	
	I change
I chose	
	I sing
I jumped	
	I write
I stopped	
I fell	
I moved	
	I work
I opened	
	I spill
I thought	
I bought	
	I bite
I called	

Can you think of some other verbs and their different tenses? Make a list on the back of this sheet.

Past to future

These sentences are written in the past tense.
☐ Rewrite them in the present and future tenses.

Yesterday Sam went to school.

Today _____

Tomorrow _____

Yesterday he walked to school.

Today _____

Tomorrow _____

Yesterday I ate my lunch.

Today _____

Tomorrow _____

Yesterday I had a banana.

Today _____

Tomorrow _____

☐ Now try some of your own past to future sentences.

Investigating verbs

Objective
Learn to consider the functions of verbs in sentences

Language issues
In this unit children revisit material they have been introduced to throughout the half-term. They look at the way in which verbs are essential components of sentences and consider the links between various verbs. The process of selecting the most appropriate verb in the right context underpins this section.

One of the outcomes of working on verbs with children can be a change in the verbs they select in their own writing. Alongside this unit teachers should be looking with children at the writing they engage in throughout the day and across the curriculum.

Ways of teaching
The idea underpinning this unit is that every sentence needs a verb and the selection of that verb makes a difference to the whole sentence. By looking at the verbless sentences the necessity of the verb to convey the overall meaning is re-emphasized. The children look at links between verbs and at the use of specific verbs in a classic text.

About the activities
Photocopiable: Can't ** without one
Children can look at these sentences to find where they think a verb could be inserted and decide what verb it could be. They can then compare their results. There will probably be a consistent response to the question where the verbs should be placed but there may be some variety in the verbs that are selected. This could lead to discussion about the type of verb we usually employ to describe an action. For example, 'The girl ** a goal' could be 'The girl scored a goal' but probably not 'The girl made a goal'.

Photocopiable:Verb to verb
By linking the verbs children revisit the familial nature of verbs and begin to explore the links between various verbs.

Photocopiable: Looking at a story
Children can share in the reading of this text from Oscar Wilde's *The Selfish Giant*. Children can
❑ find the verbs in the passage
❑ look at the verbs that are used and suggest alternatives that could have been used
❑ consider the effects of the particular verb used.

The passage has been selected because of the careful use of verbs in describing the various actions.

Following up
Redrafting: Children can look at samples of writing they have done in order to focus upon the following redrafting activity:
❑ Find a verb you have used. Can you think of two other verbs that could have been placed in that context? Which verb will you select as the best for that context? Can you explain why you chose that verb?

Collecting verbs: Children can maintain a collection of verbs that fit within the families explored in 'Verb to verb'. Charts or pages in a loose leaf folder can be maintained, to which new examples of verbs under each heading can be added, as children encounter new examples in various texts.

Can't ** without one!

❑ Each of these sentences has a verb missing.
Can you guess what it is and mark where it should go?

| The chicken away from the fox. | I my lost keys. |

| The girl a goal. | The boy into the swimming pool. |

The sun shining.

| A bird up into a tree. | Can you me a story? |

| The red monster the green monster. | We pictures of our faces. |

The cow the grass.

| Yesterday it Tuesday. | The man the car. |

Can you write your own verbless sentences for your friends to try and solve?

_____

_____

_____

_____

Verb to verb

The verbs below are all connected into families: there are different words linked to speaking, to seeing, to holding and to falling.

❏ Can you draw lines between verbs to join the families?

whispered   glimpsed   held   tumble   saw   clasped

clapped eyes on   said   clutched   stumbled   stated   kept

shouted   spotted   gripped   toppled   noticed   grabbed

observed   shrieked   clung onto   tripped   made out

plunged   grasped   expressed   collapsed   discussed

plummeted   spied   tugged   talked   looked   told

❏ Collect the different families together and write the verbs in the boxes.

Speaking	Seeing	Holding	Falling

Looking at a story

"I believe the Spring has come at last," said the Giant; and he jumped out of bed and looked out.

What did he see?

He saw a most wonderful sight. Through a little hole in the wall the children had crept in, and they were sitting in the branches of the trees. In every tree that he could see there was a little child. And the trees were so glad to have the children back again that they had covered themselves with blossoms, and were waving their arms gently above the children's heads. The birds were flying about twittering with delight, and the flowers were looking up through the green grass and laughing. It was a lovely scene, only in one corner it was still winter.

Oscar Wilde: The Selfish Giant

Marking sentences

Contents of Term 1b

Unit 1:
Basic punctuation

Consolidate understanding of sentence punctuation

Unit 2:
Commas and inverted commas

Learn to use commas in lists and inverted commas

Unit 3:
Presenting sentences

Identify and investigate a range of devices for presenting texts

Unit 4:
Sentences

Use awareness of grammar to understand sentences

Unit 5:
Working with sentences

Consolidate an understanding of sentences

This half-term

The half-term takes a basic look at sentences, concentrating largely upon the punctuation of sentences. It builds upon the elementary punctuation, demarcating sentences with capital letters and full stops or question marks, and examines the uses of inverted commas and commas in lists. The two are very different. Children tend to find inverted commas (or 'speech marks') much easier to place – after all, they demarcate a distinctive element of a sentence. The use of commas can seem much vaguer. During this half-term, children are introduced to the way in which commas separate items in a list.

Poster notes

Punctuation
The list of punctuation marks encountered in the unit is complemented by a list of sentences. In the various sentences children will find examples of the punctuation marks referred to in the list.

Font style
The poster gives a basic list of styles in which text can be printed along with some sizes of text using standard point sizes (N.B. If the poster is enlarged, these point sizes will be distorted). Children can use this as they discuss texts such as leaflets, picking out the different styles and estimating the size of typefaces they encounter.

Punctuation

- the capital letter

The children were messing about.

- the full stop

We made spinners at school.

- the question mark

How do you make a spinner**?**

- commas in lists

To make a spinner you will need paper, sticky tape, string and tissue paper.

- speech marks

Sam said "Don't jump on the settee."

- the exclamation mark

Don't jump on the settee**!**

Font style

normal text **bold text** *italic text*

CAPITALIZED TEXT

large print

small print

8 point
12 point
16 point
24 point
36 point
48 point

Basic punctuation

Objective
Consolidate understanding of sentence punctuation

Language issues
The items of punctuation covered in this unit are the capital letter, the full stop, the question mark and commas in lists. (The capital letter is, strictly speaking, not a punctuation mark, but is taught at the same time as the full stop.) Children may also demonstrate awareness of speech marks and exclamation marks.

Punctuation emerges through children's writing as it develops. Children will often write sentences that should include certain items of punctuation but omit the actual marks. The emphasis in this unit is upon activities that help to draw out the individual child's awareness of punctuation.

Ways of teaching
The items of punctuation covered in these activities link to the *National Literacy Strategy* guidelines for Key Stage 1. This unit presents an opportunity for children to revise and consolidate their awareness of punctuation.

About the activities
The sentences provided on the photocopiable page will accommodate the use of capitals, full stops, question marks, commas, inverted commas and an exclamation mark.

Photocopiable: The hot seat
As children provide responses in this activity they need a reminder of the request that they answer in sentences. A sentence can be defined as 'a unit of written language which makes sense on its own'. Children encounter this definition in their responses. If a child responds to the

first question with 'Rafi' it is a word alone and doesn't say anything. A sentence reply ('My name is Rafi') makes sense in its own right and so fits the definition. Children can check if their answers make sense in themselves and use this as a way of indicating whether or not each answer is a sentence.

Photocopiable: Recycle the words
This activity gives children the opportunity to devise sentences of their own. The words in the bins can be used to produce demarcated examples and children can bear in mind the various types of demarcation they can use. The results can be compared to look at how children used their words.

Following up
Punctuation finding: Children can look through various texts to find the different types of punctuation used. Can they figure out from these contexts the functions of various punctuation marks (such as parentheses)?

Question setting: Children can follow on from the 'Hot seat' activity setting their own questions for others in the class to answer. A questions board can be established on which children can pin a question they could put to a member of the class. A variation of this activity is to ask children to look at the board and answer a chosen number of questions that it poses.

Recycles: The recycled words activity can be adapted to use a new set of words. This can work well if vocabulary from a particular topic is included (such as gravity, force). Children then use their developing subject knowledge to devise a set of questions.

Check these out

❑ Look at these pieces of writing. Find where the punctuation marks should go. Write the sentences with the correct punctuation.

i can see my friend

_____

can we go to the park

_____

is it raining

_____

we are going to the park

_____

my favourite colours are red purple pink and orange

_____

stacey said race you to the corner

_____

can you see my friend

_____

i said boo to my mum

_____

stop look listen before you cross the road

_____

The hot seat

❑ Read the questions and write your answers in sentences.

What is your name?

_____

Where do you live?

_____

What are your favourite colours?

_____

What is your favourite place?

_____

Where did you go last weekend?

_____

What is the last programme you saw on television?

_____

What do you like doing at school?

_____

Where is your favourite place?

_____

What do you like about your favourite place?

_____

Can you write some questions to ask your friends?

_____

_____

_____

_____

Recycle the words

These words have been thrown away. Can you use the words in each bin to make a new sentence? Say each sentence aloud then write down some of them.

Commas and inverted commas

Objective
Learn to use commas in lists and inverted commas

Language issues
Within sentences, commas and speech marks form two of the most basic units of punctuation. Speech marks, or inverted commas, are used to demarcate speech in written text. They appear in pairs around the actual words spoken.

Within speech marks the first word spoken is demarcated by a capital letter. In a sentence like: 'Sam said "Don't jump on the settee"' the first spoken word is a capital. However, if the speech is broken, as in: '"Don't," said Sam, "jump on the settee"' the second part of the speech does not begin with a capital.

Among other uses, commas are used to separate items in lists, as in: 'To make a spinner you will need paper, sticky tape, string and tissue paper.' In this context, they are not usually used after the penultimate item in a list.

Ways of teaching
Once children are clear about the demarcation of sentences they can start looking at items to demarcate *within* sentences. Speech marks and commas in lists form two clear examples they can identify.

About the activities
Photocopiable: Speech shading
In this activity, the children identify speech in texts.

The texts for this activity are taken from: the scene in which Farmer Duck discovers he is free from the tyranny

of the farmer in *Farmer Duck* by Martin Waddell (Walker); the meeting of Eddie and the Bear, each carrying the other's teddy in *Where's My Teddy?* by Jez Alborough (Walker); the conversation amongst the owls left alone from *Owl Babies* by Martin Waddell (Walker).

All of these are available as Big Books.

Photocopiable: Lists with commas
By creating the normal lists and sentence lists requested in this activity children will put the idea of commas in lists into practice. Some may want to try making sentences with lists at the start, as in: 'Red, green and blue are my favourite colours.'

Photocopiable: You will need
Taking some straightforward examples, this activity asks children to look at the format of sentence lists and try making their own.

Following up
Story speech: Children can try using the speech from picture books like *Farmer Duck* to create a short drama piece acting out the story. Point out that they can find their lines for their drama by looking for the spoken words demarcated in the text.

Procedural texts: Looking at various sorts of procedural texts, children can look to see how the 'You will need' bit is organized. They could find some that are organized as lists and remodel them as sentences.

Speech shading

❏ Look at these passages from stories.
Some of these words were said by characters in the story.
For example, in

> *The duck answered "Quack!".*

the duck said the word.

❏ Using a colouring pencil, gently shade over the words that were
actually spoken.

The duck awoke and waddled wearily into the yard expecting to hear,
How goes the work?
But nobody spoke!
Then the cow and the sheep and the hens came back.
Quack? asked the duck.
Moo! said the cow.
Baa! said the sheep.
Cluck! said the hens.
Which told the duck the whole story.

    Farmer Duck *by Martin Waddell*

MY TED! gasped the bear.
A BEAR! screamed Eddy.
A BOY! yelled the bear.
MY TEDDY! cried Eddy.

    Where's My Teddy? *by Jez Alborough*

One night they woke up and their owl mother was GONE.
Where's Mummy? asked Sarah.
Oh my goodness! said Percy.
I want my Mummy! said Bill.
The baby owls thought
(all owls think a lot) -
I think she's gone hunting, said Sarah.
To get us our food! said Percy.
I want my mummy! said Bill.

    Owl Babies *by Martin Waddell*

Lists with commas

❑ Look at this list.

To make a cake you need:
Flour
Butter
Sugar
Eggs

It can be written as a sentence.

To make a cake you need flour, butter, sugar and eggs.

❑ Look at the commas. They can separate items in a list. You don't need a comma to separate the last two items in the list. The word 'and' is doing this.

❑ Try making your own lists of these groups. Write **four** each.

teachers	**tasty foods**	**farmyard animals**	**points on the compass**
	things you have in your classroom	**things you can do at playtime**	

❑ Turn your lists into sentences.

Four of our teachers are _____

Four tasty foods are _____

Four farmyard animals are _____

Four points of the compass are _____

In our classroom we have _____

At playtime we can _____

❑ Try making up some sentence lists about other things. Here are some ideas to get you started.

places to go	**people in your family**	**things you can do**
names you like	**good television programmes**	
things you can make	**colours**	**favourite sweets**

You will need

❑ Look at these lists of things you will need for various activities.

> To make a cake you will need flour, eggs, sugar and vanilla essence.

> To make a kite you will need plain paper, tissue paper, string and sticky tape.

> To play 'Pin the tail on the donkey' you will need a blindfold, a pin, a large sheet of paper and a thick felt tip pen.

❑ Try devising your own.

To_____ you will need_____

To_____ you will need_____

To_____ you will need_____

To_____ you will need_____

To_____ you will need_____

To_____ you will need_____

> Don't forget to separate things with a comma.

Presenting sentences

Objective
Identify and investigate a range of devices for presenting texts

Language issues
There are a variety of ways in which text can be arranged and formatted to communicate with a reader in a particular way. The use of different print sizes, the printing of letters as capitals or in italicized or bold type can result in different types of emphasis on certain words.

As access to word processors has increased, use of these various devices has permeated all sorts of writing and is a common feature of the production of notices and newsletters.

Ways of teaching
By collecting examples of different text types children can acquire some insight into the varied purposes they serve. This is one of those areas where, once children have started looking for examples, they keep on finding them.

About the activities
Photocopiable: Leaflets
While this unit relies upon children looking at a selection of real leaflets, the examples on the photocopiable page are designed in a way that uses the various text types noted above.

Photocopiable: Typefaces and texts
Looking at various text types should involve children in considering the effect the varied examples have upon a reader. This activity engages children in the task of evaluating such effects.

Photocopiable: Design your own leaflets
Children can make up the event for which they will produce a leaflet or devise one that advertises a real event, such as a party or a class assembly.

Following up
Grouping: Collect a large number of leaflets and cut out the different typefaces found on them. Ask the children to group the typefaces into sets. They can devise their own criteria or use the test types looked at in this unit. They may attempt to define their own criteria for grouping a certain type of text, such as 'It looks swirly'!

Word processing: This unit presents an opportunity to support children in their use of the word processor. They can look at the various ways in which IT enables them to manipulate text.

Real leaflets: There may be some real events in the school calendar for which children could devise the leaflet or letter home. These could be done on the computer.

Leaflets

❑ Look at these leaflets and find examples of
bold text
italic text
capitalized text
large print
small print

The Ultimate CD Fair

HUNDREDS OF CDS. BIG VALUE. SMALL PRICES

ROCK. POP. RAP. HOUSE. JAZZ.

Don't miss it.

James Street Centre
Saturday 20th May at 1.00

Where can you find the cheapest furniture?

Only at **JACKSON'S** furniture warehouse.

The Jackson's SALE starts this week.

Quality Furniture. Pine tables. Three piece suites.

Hundreds of bargains.

Sale starts <u>Friday</u> at <u>9:00 am.</u>

Why are the different types of text used? What effect do they have?

Typefaces and texts

❑ Look at some leaflets. Cut out some of the different examples of text. Collect some of the different ways text is printed. Stick them in the Text type column. In the Description column write some notes on the text type.
Why is it printed like that? What effect does it have?

Text type	Description

Design your own leaflets

❑ Use these outlines to design your own leaflet.
What will it be for? What are the important words?
What types of text could you produce?

Sentences

Objective
Use awareness of grammar to understand sentences

Language issues
An awareness of the grammar of sentences is one of the cues readers use to decipher unfamiliar text. The reader may not know what the word 'sprigged' means but in a sentence like 'Joe sprigged the tree' their awareness of grammar should assist them to understand what class of word they are dealing with. The way the words are combined and the experience the reader brings to the text will lead them to guess 'sprigged' is a verb performed by Joe. Along with other cues such as pictures and other parts of the text readers use this understanding to help them read the unfamiliar.

Ways of teaching
Throughout this unit children encounter the idea of certain types of words taking up certain places in sentences. This can be supported by covering over words in a shared text and asking children to guess what the covered word could be. While children may guess the exact word, an important part of this activity is teaching children which words could possibly fit such gaps and which will not make sense.

About the activities
Photocopiable: Possible words
As they cut out the words that fit the sentences in this activity children can look to see which space they could fit within the sentence. It is worth stressing to children that they need to cut and place all the words in a particular sentence before sticking words down as some of the individual words could fit more than one space.

Photocopiable: Rebuild the sentence
As children rebuild the sentences on this sheet they may vary the word order. For example, one may produce 'We helped carry the chairs to the caretaker' and another 'We helped the caretaker to carry the chairs'. The variations could provide material for a discussion over which ones make sense and which ones don't.

Photocopiable: Catch the meaning
As children hazard guesses to the meanings of words the teacher may want to discuss exactly what it is that underpins such guesses. Do they guess the meaning on the basis of the sound of the word? Does likeness to other words play a part?

Following up
Blank game: Children can listen to sentences from which a word has been omitted, such as 'I sharpened the _____' and each write their guess as to what the missing word might be on a piece of paper. They must not let anyone else see what they are writing but once everyone has recorded their guess they can find others who have proposed the same word as their own. The result should be little clusters forming of children who guessed the same word. The teacher can then reveal the original.

New words chart: Keep a chart in the classroom of unfamiliar words that children encounter as they read. Record the full sentence but circle the unfamiliar word. Encourage children to add to the chart as they read. The class can share in the task of looking through the chart and suggesting meanings for the unfamiliar.

Possible words

Each of these sentences is incomplete. Can you find the missing word or words in the word bin?

❏. Rewrite the sentences correctly on the back of this sheet.

The farmer ——— the sheep and there —— ten in the ———

Tom made — mess in the Art Corner so — teacher told him to ——— —— ——

I lost my ——— but then found ——— under — table.

were field counted	tidy it up a his	them keys the

The —— was sinking so everyone —— to ——.

I played on my ——— until it —— time for ———.

We —— to the ——— and it ——— with rain.

had swim boat	bed computer was	beach poured went

Anisa came to — house and we ——— chips for ———.

The ——— listened — the radio and ——— to their favourite ———.

I ——— to the ——— and ——— on the ———.

had tea my	to children song danced	played swings park went

Rebuild the sentence

❑ Rebuild the mixed up sentences. Make sure you use every word.

cinema
films.   I
love
to watch
cartoon
to   the
going

name?
is
What
your

o' clock.
news   My
six   always
watches
at   the
mum

helped
carry   the
chairs.
caretaker
to   We
the

can
I
bridge
see the

at   hill.
very   the
steep
school   a
is   top
of   Our

_____

_____

_____

_____

_____

Catch the meaning

You don't have to recognize a word to guess what it could mean.
❏ Look at these sentences.

The boy slipped and cascaded down the stairs.
"Oh no, I have made a colossal mistake"
The children were naughty and forfeited their playtime.
The nasty boy was saying pernicious things.
The secret club held a clandestine meeting.
He cleaned the window until it was immaculate.
"Help! Help!" she bellowed.
I said a rude word and scandalized my family.
The boat quietly sailed over a tranquil lake.
The fly buzzed around the room and was a vexation.

❏ Now look at the words in this table. Write what you think the words mean.

Word	Posssble meaning
cascaded	
colossal	
forfeited	
pernicious	
clandestine	
immaculate	
bellowed	
scandalized	
tranquil	
vexation	

❏ When you have finished, look the words up in the dictionary and check your guesses.

Working with sentences

Objective
Consolidate an understanding of sentences

Language issues
Sentences can take many forms. There are *simple* sentences in which a single clause says one thing, such as: 'The dog chased the cat.'

There are *complex* sentences, in which another clause develops part of a simple sentence, such as: 'The dog, having finished scratching his fleas, chased the cat.'Refer to the subject knowledge section on page 148.

Compound sentences feature two or more clauses that are equal in significance, linked by a connective like 'and' or 'then', such as: 'The dog chased the cat and the cow jumped over the moon.'

Minor sentences don't always look like sentences but, in a text, they stand alone and perform a function. Examples include: 'Oh no!' and 'Hello there!'

Ways of teaching
Teachers have found various ways of defining sentences for children. The problem is that some of these definitions are open to interpretation. Some definitions of a sentence are too technical to introduce to children of Key Stage 2 age. Teachers may have to rely on their instincts when deciding whether constructions which the children write are indeed sentences. The old-fashioned definition – that a sentence is capable of standing on its own and making sense – is a useful one.

About the activities
Photocopiable: Strange sentences
Using the words on the photocopiable page, children have to try and write a sentence. They can aim to create the strangest sentence, possibly even voting on which one is strangest of all.

Photocopiable: Sentence starts, sentence ends
This activity develops children's growing awareness of when a sentence should start and finish. They have to try and find, within the printed text, the points at which sentences will start and finish. Once they have done this they can compare their results to see how they have judged sentence starts and endings.

Photocopiable: Making sentences
As they place the lines of text shown on the photocopiable page into sentences children will be faced with the task of creating some longer sentences than they may have encountered before. Some of the lines of text, such as 'I can read', are sentences in themselves. However, as they build new sentences out of such lines they may start creating complex and compound sentences.

Following up
Depunctuate a text: Looking at a text on the word processor, children can remove the punctuation. This will involve finding all the marks that demarcate the sentences in some way and deleting them or, in the case of capital letters, changing the case.

Sentence facts: Children can look for things like the longest and shortest sentence they can encounter. They can draw on sayings and jokes to try and collect their favourite sentences, taking lines out of poetry and drawing on well known quotations.

Strange sentences

❏ Look at the words in the word bins and try to include each set of words in a sentence.

gorilla
slippers
ate

_____

_____

reading
singing
made

_____

_____

stopped
underwater
coat

_____

_____

moon
send
tree

_____

_____

teacher
dinner
purple
disgusting

_____

_____

found
turned
magic
coin

_____

_____

can
balloon
gone
animals

_____

Sentence starts, sentence ends

❑ Look at these pieces of writing. There are no capital letters or full stops.
Can you see the sentences in the passages?

last Tuesday I went to the park
I played on the swings my
friend came and played with me
when it was time to go I asked
my friend if she wanted to
come to my house my friend
said "yes" but first she had to
ask her mum after she asked
her mum she came to my house
she stayed for tea

my mum did a parachute jump
she had never done one before
her friend dared her to do it she
was very scared but she went to
all the lessons on the day of her
parachute jump we all went to
watch her we saw her jump out of
the plane we waited and then her
parachute opened we were so
proud of her

once upon a time there was a
princess she lived all alone in a
big castle every day she went
to the market and bought two
baskets of fruit one basket

was full of apples the other
was full of oranges that was
all she had for breakfast
and dinner and tea

❑ Using colouring pencils, lightly shade over each sentence in a different colour.

Making sentences

None of these lines of text has a capital letter or a full stop. Some of them could be sentences. Some of them are not.

❏ Cut them out and sort the ones that could be sentences from the ones that couldn't. Remember that a sentence stands on its own and says something.

and in the room at the bottom of the stairs there was

can make a lot of things

we can read a book at the end of the day

I went to the jumble sale and bought some games

Serena didn't go straight home after school

I can read

so that was not a problem

look at this hole in the road

if we use all these boxes we can make a castle

on Tuesday we are going to

what do you know about a

the pirate lost his parrot

❏ Look at the collection of slips that do not make a sentence. Can you suggest sentences in which they would fit?

Adjectives

Contents of Term 2a

Unit 1:
What is an adjective?
Define the function of adjectives

Unit 2:
Identifying adjectives
Identify adjectives

Unit 3:
Changing adjectives
Experiment with substituting adjectives in sentences

Unit 4:
Classifying adjectives
Collect and classify adjectives

Unit 5:
Experimenting with adjectives
Experiment with substitution and the impact of different adjectives

This half-term

The focus of this half-term is upon adjectives. After being introduced and defined, it is important that children experience their use in context. For this reason the unit contains a large number of text-based activities looking at a range of texts from poems to chocolate bars.

Poster notes

Adjectives
The poster provides a list of various types of adjectives, and can be used as a way of introducing adjectives, as well as in activities in which children use or classify various adjectives.

The Listeners
The poem, 'The Listeners' by Walter de la Mare, features in the 'Find the adjective in…' activity. The full text is reprinted here. The poem contains a mysterious text that children will be able to follow, but one that is rich with interesting and poetic adjectives.

Adjectives

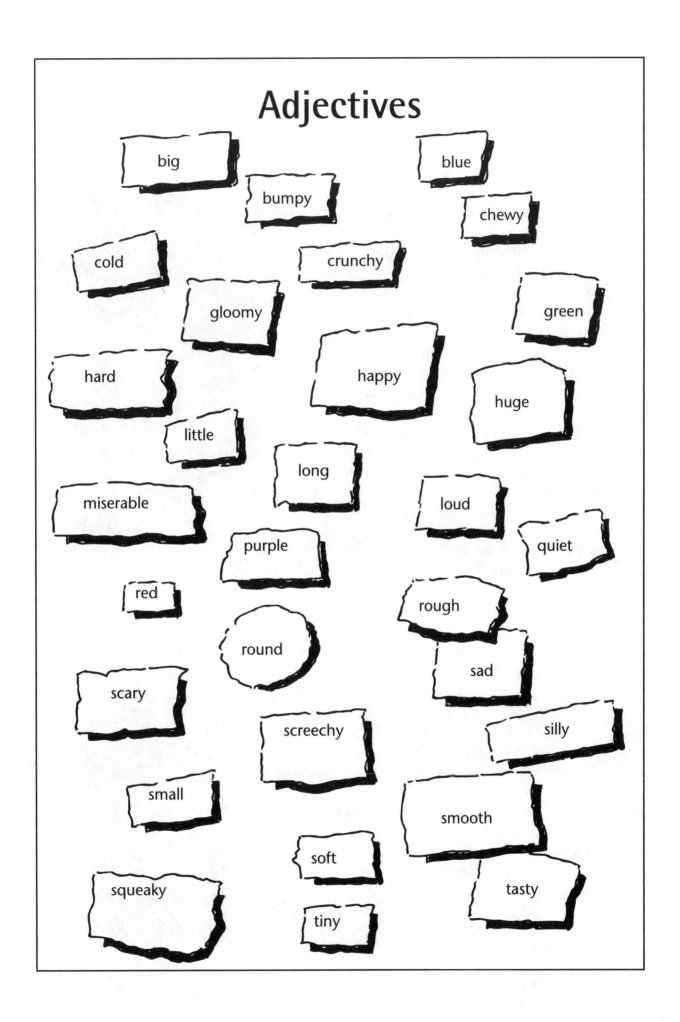

big

blue

bumpy

chewy

cold

crunchy

gloomy

green

hard

happy

huge

little

long

loud

miserable

purple

quiet

red

rough

round

sad

scary

screechy

silly

small

smooth

soft

tasty

squeaky

tiny

The Listeners

'Is there anybody there?' said the Traveller,
  Knocking on the moonlit door;
And his horse in the silence champed the grasses
  Of the forest's ferny floor:
And a bird flew up out of the turret,
  Above the Traveller's head:
And he smote upon the door again a second time;
  'Is there anybody there?' he said.
But no one descended to the Traveller;
  No head for the leaf-fring'd sill
Leaned over and looked into his grey eyes,
  Where he stood perplexed and still.
But only a host of phantom listeners
  That dwelt in the lone house then
Stood listening in the quiet of the moonlight
  To that voice from the world of men:
Stood thronging the faint moonbeams on the dark stair,
  That goes down to the empty hall,
Hearkening in an air stirred and shaken
  By the lonely Traveller's call.
And he felt in his heart their strangeness,
  Their stillness answering his cry,
While his horse moved, cropping the dark turf,
  'Neath the starred and leafy sky;
For he suddenly smote on the door, even
  Louder, and lifted his head: –
'Tell them I came, and no one answered,
  That I kept my word,' he said.
Never the least stir made the listeners,
  Though every word he spake
Fell echoing through the shadowiness of the still house
  From the one man left awake:
Ay, they heard his foot upon the stirrup,
  And the sound of iron on stone,
And how the silence surged slowly backward,
  When the plunging hoofs were gone.

Walter de la Mare

What is an adjective?

Objective
Define the function of adjectives

Language issues
Adjectives describe or modify nouns. In sentences like 'The big dog chased me' and 'Today is a sunny day', the words 'big' and 'sunny' modify the noun.

Adjectives can come before a noun, as in 'the red book'; such adjectives are called *attributive*. Adjectives can also come after a noun, as in 'The dog is fierce'; these are called *predicative* adjectives. Most adjectives can be both attributive or predicative, depending upon the context. However, an adjective like 'mere' is only used in an attributive way whereas an adjective like 'abroad' is only used in a predicative way.

Ways of teaching
For children with a developing vocabulary adjectives are something of an extra to the sense of sentences. They could get by with 'The dog chased me'. However, teachers should be striving to develop the children's use of language to include the elaboration entailed in modifying nouns to create sentences like 'The big dog chased me'.

About the activities
Photocopiable: Using adjectives
As an initial activity, this photocopiable page asks children to think of words they would use to describe the nouns shown. Once they have completed these it may be interesting to compare their results to see whether any common adjectives have been applied to particular nouns.

Photocopiable: Qualifying the noun
Attributive adjectives precede nouns and modify them. In this activity children look at the illustrations and try to think of a word they would use to describe the noun shown in the illustration.

Photocopiable: Adjectives in texts
To undertake this activity children will need to be equipped with a range of texts that they can cut up, such as comics, newspapers, leaflets and so on. This activity sets them off on a search for different adjectives.

Following up
Collecting: Once they have been introduced to adjectives children can start a collection of various examples. These can be recorded along with the noun that each one modifies.

Shared reading: During shared reading activities, children can look out for adjectives. The discovery of new adjectives needs to be coupled with looking for the noun they modify.

Using adjectives

❑ Make up some story characters. In the spaces below draw your characters and write some words that describe them. Is your monster 'scary' or 'sensible'?

Devise a monster...   Devise a robot...

_____   _____

_____   _____

_____   _____

_____   _____

Devise a dragon...   Devise a wizard...

_____   _____

_____   _____

_____   _____

Qualifying the noun

❑ Look at the objects below. In the spaces underneath think of a word that could tell us what the object is like, for example, the *thin* hand, the *slender* hand.

the _____ hand   the _____ monster   the _____ spaceship

the _____ day   the _____ star   the _____ cat

the _____ ring   the _____ dog   the _____ fire

the _____ mug   the _____ house   the _____ ball

the _____ pirate   the _____ bath   the _____ bird

the _____ snake   the _____ mouse   the _____ music

the _____ baby   the _____ dress   the _____ elephant

Adjectives in texts

❑ Collect some examples of sentences with adjectives. Stick or copy them into the sentence column in the table. What are the adjectives describing? What description are they making?

Sentence	What is being described?	How is it described?
This charming house is situated on a quiet street.	the house the street	charming quiet

Identifying adjectives

Objective
Identify adjectives

Language issues
One of the main ways in which adjectives can be identified is to look for the nouns that they modify. Adjectives describe nouns and, while they may come in an attributive or predicative position, the understanding of adjectives is usually dependent upon an awareness of the noun they are modifying.

Words that are not usually thought of as adjectives can perform an adjectival function, so a word like 'sitting' while usually seen as a verb, can be used in a context like 'a sitting duck' or 'sitting tenant' to modify a noun.

Ways of teaching
The identification of adjectives is something that has to be taught in conjunction with the function of adjectives (see Unit 1). The aim of this unit is that children look at words that are modifying nouns. The term 'modify' may or may not be used in the classroom but the idea should underpin work on this aspect of grammar.

About the activities
Photocopiable: Find the adjective in...
As a stimulus to this activity children can look at texts they are working on or a text shared in class, and apply the 'Adjectives in texts' photocopiable from Unit 1. They can look through the texts printed here for examples of adjectives and look beyond these to other texts.

Photocopiable: Descriptive spaces
This activity works on the type of changes adjectives make in a sentence. Each of the printed sentences works well on its own but can be added to by inserting adjectives. Children can begin to understand where adjectives get placed and the sorts of changes they make.

Photocopiable: Adjectives in poems
Poetry can provide a rich resource for finding the uses of adjectives. The examples shown should act as a starting point from which children can explore other examples.

Following up
Fields of adjectives: Children can collect similar leaflets and promotional material such as estate agent leaflets, holiday brochures and prize-draw junk mail. The main thing is to begin with publications that have a common thread. They can look through these and see which adjectives commonly appear in these materials.

Adjectives in pictures: Looking at pictures, whether they be photos from magazines or paintings in a gallery, children can look at items in the picture and think of the adjective they would use to describe them. They need to name something or someone in the picture and decide on an adjective that describes the noun.

Selling properties: Children can produce their own estate agent leaflet or holiday brochure. They could try describing their own house or make a leaflet for the sale of the school. They could produce a promotional paragraph describing the locality for example.

Find the adjective in...

❑ Look at these texts. In each of them, circle the words or phrases that are adjectives.

 This spacious house is situated on a charming, quiet road.

(Estate agent mailing)

 On top of a windy hill with nothing else to be friends with lived
Something Else

(K. Cave 'Something Else')

 I took Dad's watch to pieces.
Mum said that I could.
I love these shiny wheels and things...

('The Watch Mender' by Michael Glover)

 'Is there anybody there?' said the Traveller,
Knocking on the moonlit door

('The Listeners' by Walter de la Mare)

 Moist tender coconut covered in thick milk chocolate.

('Bounty' advert)

 Torrential rains have caused a flood alert across the region.

(Local paper)

 He receives comfort like cold porridge.

(*The Tempest*)

 Don't miss this new series of scary stories.

 Thank you for the fantastic present. It was a brilliant surprise.

Can you write some other sentences using these adjectives?

Descriptive spaces

❑ Read these sentences.
Where could you place an adjective in each sentence? Could you place more than one adjective in each sentence?
❑ Draw arrows in the spaces where you could put adjectives. Which ones would you add? The first one is done for you.

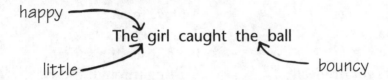

The bear hid behind a tree

The boat crossed the river

The wolf chased the duck

The boy went on the bus to the shop

My friend lives in a house in my street

On the table at the party there was a cake

The goblin lived in a den under the bridge

The spaceship landed on the planet

Adjectives in poems

❑ Find the adjectives in this poem. How important are they when you read the poem?

Our Car

Our car's old
And very rusty.
It clangs and bangs
And rattles and
It's very dusty.
Dad's always got his head
Under the bonnet
And the roof's got lots
Of stains and dents upon it.
And in the mornings,
When it's cold,
It doesn't like starting,
And just coughs,
And coughs, and coughs…
But when I'm
In the back seat,
Strapped in, looking out,

I begin to think
I'm a racing driver,
And we're off…
And when it's dark,
I'm a spaceship captain,
Blasting through the stars.

I tell you,
I've really been far
In our old car.

Tony Bradman

❑ Collect the adjectives in this table.
What do they make you think of when you read the poem?

Adjectives	My response

Changing adjectives

Objective
Experiment with substituting adjectives in sentences

Language issues
The range of adjectives that can be used is enormous and the subtleties of the range make them fascinating words to work with. The use of 'satisfactory' rather than 'good' to describe a meal or a piece of work is just one example of the way in which different adjectives, used in different ways, carry with them varying connotations. They are loaded words!

Ways of teaching
Through experimenting with the substitution of adjectives children should develop their language use in two ways. Firstly, substitution reinforces the way in which adjectives are combined with other words and can be selected from a wide range. Secondly, substituting adjectives provides an interesting way of extending children's vocabulary. It is through substitution that children move beyond describing things merely as 'nice' to using other, more expressive words.

About the activities
Photocopiable: Alternative adjectives
Through focusing upon well-known objects children can try to list a variety of adjectives they could use to describe them.

Photocopiable: Match the adjective
This activity works backwards from various adjectives and asks children to consider which nouns could be described by them.

Photocopiable: Change the adjective
Once children have tried changing the adjectives in the text shown on the photocopiable page, they can try it with the various texts they encounter in shared and guided reading sessions.

Following up
Class thesaurus: Using published thesauruses children can look up commonly used adjectives such as 'good' and 'bad' and list alternatives that could be used. The examples could be bound into a class thesaurus.

Class rating: Children can review their own writing and each others to draw up a list of the most commonly used adjectives in their class. They could provide this auditing service to other teachers! Once they have drawn up this list they could use their class thesaurus to suggest alternatives.

Shared choice: During shared writing activities the class could experiment with the rule that they will not use an adjective until they have thought of two possibilities that could take the same place within a sentence.

Alternative adjectives

❏ Choose **eight** things you know well. Put one in the centre of each of the spiders below. At the end of each leg write an adjective to describe the thing. The first one is started for you.

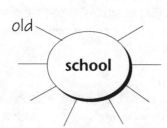

old

school

Suggestion Box

school dinners	playtime
parties	clowns
books	computer
games	home
the shop	buses.
my favourite television programme	

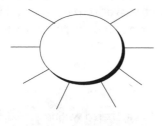

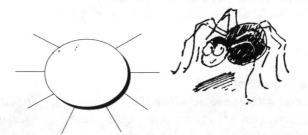

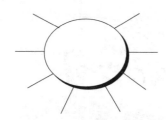

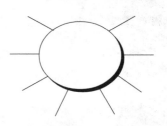

Match the adjective

❏ The slips below contain an adjective and something that the adjective describes. Can you think of **two** other things the adjective could describe? The first one is done for you.

tall			
tree	skyscraper	lampost	

small			
ant	_____	_____	

green			
traffic light	_____	_____	

loud			
jet plane	_____	_____	

fast			
comet	_____	_____	

scary			
spider	_____	_____	

soft			
tissue	_____	_____	

cold			
ice cube	_____	_____	

bright			
light bulb	_____	_____	

tasty			
chocolate	_____	_____	

Change the adjective

❑ Find the adjectives in this passage. Circle them. Can you list them and suggest other adjectives that could take their place?

A dog barks and this cat with no name scrambles up a fence. This

boy called Shane sees the little cat and yells, "Hey, you! Scaredycat!"

The cat with no name hears the loud voice of the boy. And way up

there on the top of the fence, this clever baby thing roll itself up.

Such a tight little ball of fierce cat. It growls and then it spits right

at the boy called Shane. Mad as anything!

From Way Home *by Libby Hathorn*

Adjective	Alternative adjective

Classifying adjectives

Objective
Collect and classify adjectives

Language issues
There are several different kinds of adjectives. By far the largest class of adjectives modify nouns by describing qualities such as size, shape or colour, such as 'big cat', 'round clock' and 'blue book'. There are also adjectives that modify nouns by indicating the quantity of a particular noun, for example 'lots of cats'.

Other types of words such as demonstratives (this, that), possessives (my, your) and interrogatives (which, what) can be referred to as adjectives. They too modify nouns, as in 'Look at these books' or 'Look at my books'. Numerals are also classed as adjectives (as in 'Bring me two books').

Ways of teaching
Within this unit the focus is upon categories of adjective. This is a substantial task for children but provides a means of exploring the range of adjectives available to them.

About the activities
Photocopiable: Types of adjective
This activity presents certain criteria that children can use to sort a set of adjectives. Once they have undertaken this activity they can try to adapt it, devising their own criteria for sorting adjectives. It could be as personal as 'adjectives we like' and 'adjectives we don't like'.

Photocopiable: Adjective machine
As a practice in using the adjective machine children could run the adjectives from the 'Types of adjective' activity through it.

Photocopiable: Devise the Thingy
Once they have devised and described their own 'Thingy' monsters children can look at each other's and see if they can add to one another's list of adjectives used to describe the creatures.

Following up
Guessing: Children can play a guessing game in which someone has to think of an item in the room and other children request types of adjective about the object such as 'an adjective to describe its colour' or 'an adjective to describe how clean or dirty it is'. The questions are difficult to formulate and often result in some discussion. This game can also be played using objects on a tray with the class sitting in a circle around it.

Sets: Writing various adjectives on cards the teacher can ask groups of children to devise their own criteria and sort the adjectives accordingly.

Types of adjective

❏ Read the phrases in these boxes. Each of them contains an adjective. Can you see what some of these adjectives have in common?

❏ Cut out the boxes and sort them into those that contain:
• adjectives that describe colour (such as 'red')
• adjectives that describe mood and feeling (such as 'gloomy')
• adjectives that describe size (such as 'tiny')?

A big dog	A long road	A sad boy
A wide door	A scared man	A black coat
A purple shirt	A little boy	A miserable day
A blue sea	A wild party	A red shoe
An angry dog	A small flower	A green leaf
A happy girl	An orange orange	A brown dog
A tiny spider	A calm dog	A huge boat

Adjective machine

❑ Read through some texts finding adjectives.
Can you find some adjectives that describe
• how something looks (eg, green)
• how something feels (eg, rough)
• how something sounds (eg, loud)
• how something tastes (eg, chewy)?

❑ Write some of the words you find in these spaces.

looks	feels	sounds	tastes

Devise the Thingy

This is a Thingy.

It is a big, warty, squeaky, spotted, smelly Thingy.

Can you invent **four** new Thingies? For each Thingy you need **at least three** adjectives.

Could you give your Thingies names? Could you use them in a story?

Experimenting with adjectives

Objective
Experiment with substitution and the impact of different adjectives

Language issues
As was noted in the previous unit, adjectives can be 'loaded' words. They are more open to the opinion of the language-user than almost any other type of word (together with adverbs). A dog can be referred to as a 'mutt' or a 'pooch', varying the noun used, but the subjective judgements involved in the use of adjectives present a wider range of possibilities, including 'a nice dog', 'a nasty dog', 'a fierce dog' or 'a smelly dog'.

Ways of teaching
As children encounter adjectives they sometimes begin to create their own and experiment in various ways with the describing of nouns. Examples such as the child who described the local fried chicken shop as 'pepperish' illustrate the way in which children will try to create or track down the descriptive word that has the right impact. In this unit children experiment with various adjectives, noticing the particular impact of each example.

About the activities
Photocopiable: In your own words
This activity involves children looking at pieces of their own writing. As preparation, the teacher may want to select pieces of writing that would best be applied to this activity.

Photocopiable: Similar adjectives
As a means of exploring the varying impacts of, and connections between certain adjectives, this activity clusters like with like, asking children to group adjectives together with the words shown.

Photocopiable: Chocolate bar
This activity is best done after a week or two spent collecting real chocolate bar wrappers and looking at the slogans on them. A list could be kept of some of the best examples.

Following up
Drafting partnerships: Children can work in pairs reading one another's writing and noting places where they could have used particular adjectives and the impact of their chosen ones. In this way the children reading their partners' writing act as critics, exploring the impact various adjectives have upon them.

Advertise: Following on from the work done on chocolate bars children can try devising their own slogan for a different product. It could be an item of food or an organization of which they are a member.

In your own words

❑ Look at some pieces of writing you have done. Find some sentences that could have contained adjectives. Write the sentences in the first column.

❑ Write each sentence again. This time, put in any adjectives that will make a better sentence.

Original	Redraft

Similar adjectives

❑ Look at the adjectives at the top of each box.
Can you think of **three** other adjectives that are similar? You might find some on
the 'Adjectives' poster.

red

sharp

sour

unhappy

small

Chocolate bar

❏ Look at the chocolate bar below then try to devise two of your own. Notice the slogan that uses an adjective to describe the chocolate bar.

Nouns and pronouns

Contents of Term 2b

This half-term

The main focus of this half-term is upon nouns and pronouns. In particular there is a look at the ways in which plural nouns are formed from singulars and the way in which person, in the grammatical sense of the term, affects the way sentences read. The half-term leads on to an examination of the essential words in a sentence and the way in which the position in a sentence gives a clue to the meaning of a word.

Poster notes

Making plurals
This poster provides a reference point throughout the half-term, but particularly in Unit 1. The table is used in the unit to show the ways in which plurals are made. The point to stress is that the usual rule is to add 's' to a noun to make a plural but that there are exceptions to this rule. The poster should be kept on display for children to refer to as they form plurals in their independent work.

Collective nouns
The poster provides a list of collective nouns and will support work in Unit 2. Some are better known than others. Children can draw on examples on the poster while adding to their repertoire of collective nouns.

Making plurals

Singular ends	Usual rule	Examples
'y' after a consonant	Remove 'y'. Add 'ies'	fairy → fairies
'o' after a consonant	add 'es'	potato → potatoes
with a sound like 's' such as 's', 'sh', 'tch', 'x', 'z'	add 'es'	kiss → kisses wish → wishes watch → watches
'ch' sounding like it does at the end of 'perch'	add 'es'	perch → perches

Collective nouns

a **flock** of birds

a **choir** of singers

a **hand** of bananas

a **swarm** of bees

a **deck** of cards

a **crowd** of people

a **fleet** of ships

a **herd** of cows

a **team** of footballers

a **bunch** of grapes

a **crew** of sailors

a **suit** of clothes

a **school** of whales

a **stack** of hay

a **pack** of wolves

a **staff** of teachers

a **forest** of trees

Introducing plurals

Objective
Recognize the use of singular and plural nouns

Language issues
A plural denotes more than one of a noun, whether it be a single item or a single collection of lots of items (a colective noun). The usual rule for turning a singular noun into a plural is to add an 's' (as in 'cows', 'videos' and 'pieces') but there are some exceptions to this rule. The way in which a singular noun is adapted to make a plural depends on the ending of the singular. The exceptions are as follows:

Singular ends	Usual rule	Example
'y' after a consonant	Remove 'y'. Add 'ies'	fairy → fairies
'o' after a consonant	add 'es'	potato → potatoes
with a sound like 's' such as 's', 'sh', 'tch', 'x', 'z'	add 'es'	kiss → kisses wish → wishes watch → watches
'ch' sounding like it does at the end of 'perch'	add 'es'	perch → perches

Ways of teaching
The rule of adding 's' except when faced with an exception to the rule is a key element of children learning to form plural nouns correctly. Children need to practice noticing nouns that result in exceptions.

About the activities
Photocopiable: Find the plural
As children match singular and plural nouns this activity can result in them looking for the general rule of adding an 's' and noticing some of the exceptions. The activity can be adapted by writing the singular and plural nouns on cards and asking the children to match them up (see *Cards* in 'Following up').

Photocopiable: Singular to plural
As they change these sentences, children will notice that there are certain words they need to change and certain words that stay the same.

Photocopiable: Hints about plurals
This activity provides a straightforward introduction to the effect that pluralization has on the spelling of certain words. It introduces children to the chart of exceptions to the 'add an "s"' rule.

Following up
Cards: Using the nouns on 'Find the plural' and other singular /plural nouns a set of cards can be made showing the singular and plural of a set of nouns. Children can try to match these up. As new nouns are introduced to the class they can be added to the card pack.

Shared text: As children share a text with the teacher they can look out for singular and plural nouns they encounter along the way.

Unusual plurals: Children can keep a collection of plurals that are exceptions to the 'add an "s"' rule.

Find the plural

❏ Look at these words. Find their plurals. Write them in the plural space.

Singular	Plural
child	children
fish	
woman	
mouse	
school	
house	
friend	
foot	
fox	
leaf	
potato	
class	
dress	
box	
branch	
dog	
girl	
teacher	
switch	

houses

dresses   branches

dogs   potatoes

leaves

classes

children

teachers   feet

boxes   friends

schools   fish

foxes   girls

switches

women   mice

❏ Use **three** of the singular nouns in sentences.

_____

_____

_____

❏ Use **three** of the plural nouns in sentences.

_____

_____

_____

Singular to plural

❑ Look at these sentences. The nouns are singular. Can you rewrite the sentences with plurals? You may need to change other words to suit the plurals.

The pirate talked to the parrot.	
The girl played with her football.	
The clown fell off the bike.	
My friend ate the potato.	
You use the switch to turn on the light.	
Don't lose the key for the cupboard.	
I can make a cake with a cherry on top.	
The dog chased the teacher up the tree.	
The princess found her dress in the box.	
The leaf fell from a branch of the tree.	
The girl had a sweet.	

Hints about plurals

There are different ways of turning a singular into a plural.

One way of working out how a singular is made into a plural is to look at word endings. For example, if a singular ends in 'ch' we often make the plural by adding 'es'.

Singular ends	Usual rule	Example
'y' after a consonant	Remove 'y'. Add 'ies'	fairy → fairies
'o' after a consonant	add 'es'	potato → potatoes
with a sound like 's' such as 's', 'sh', 'tch', 'x', 'z'	add 'es'	kiss → kisses wish → wishes watch → watches
'ch' sounding like it does at the end of 'perch'	add 'es'	perch → perches

❏ Try making the plurals for these words.

Singular	Plural
diary	
nappy	
tomato	
rodeo	
cross	
crutch	
church	
splash	
tray	
watch	
hutch	
porch	
hiss	
mess	
pooch	
ranch	
crash	

❏ Try finding other words that are examples of the different ways we make plurals.

Collective nouns

Objective
Understand and recognize the use of collective nouns

Language issues
Collective nouns are used to denote a group of items, such as 'a bunch of bananas' or 'a flock of sheep'. Collections are single items, but they can also be pluralized (meaning more than one collection of items), as in 'flocks of sheep'.

There is a small number of commonly used collective nouns that children will encounter.

Ways of teaching
Once children have grasped the idea of a collective noun the important element in the teaching of this aspect of grammar will be to encounter examples.

About the activities
Photocopiable: A pile of guesses
Some of these collective nouns will be known to the children. Some will require an element of guesswork. The correct pairings are:

Photocopiable: Make up collective nouns
As children create their own collective nouns they can look at the ways in which their chosen collective terms suit the nouns concerned.

Photocopiable: Find the collections
As already noted, familiarity with examples is a useful way of learning how collective nouns work. Through seeking out the examples and matching them together children review some of the collective nouns they have encountered in this unit.

Following up
Quiz: Children can make a quiz out of collective nouns and put them to adults to test their knowledge of this aspect of grammar.

Collection: As they read shared texts, listen to people talking and view various media, children can stay on the lookout for other examples of collective nouns.

Collective noun	Noun
a flock of	birds
a crowd of	people
a bunch of	grapes
a team of	footballers
a swarm of	bees
a herd of	cows
a hand of	bananas
a choir of	singers
a crew of	sailors
a litter of	puppies
a deck of	cards
a school of	whales
a staff of	teachers
a suit of	clothes
a stack of	hay
a pack of	wolves
a forest of	trees
a fleet of	ships

A pile of guesses

Collective nouns name collections.

The name of a collection of sheep is a 'flock'.

'Flock' is a collective noun.
❑ Look at the collective nouns. Cut them out and match them to the things they collect.

Collective nouns		Nouns	
a flock of	a litter of	trees	clothes
a crowd of	a deck of	singers	sailors
a bunch of	a school of	whales	wolves
a team of	a staff of	ships	cows
a swarm of	a suit of	birds	cards
a herd of	a stack of	bees	bananas
a hand of	a pack of	grapes	teachers
a choir of	a forest of	puppies	people
a crew of	a fleet of	hay	footballers

❑ Compare your results with a friend.

Make up collective nouns

Here are some things for which we couldn't find collective nouns! Can you make up collective nouns for them? You might use a word you already know (such as a *noise* of teachers). You could make one up (such as a *moanmoanmoan* of teachers). You could use a collective noun you already know (such as a *swarm* of teachers).

A _____

of slugs

A _____

of teachers

A _____

of school dinners

A _____

of smelly socks

A _____

of dentists

A _____

of monsters

A _____

of fairies

A _____

of aliens

A _____

of puddles

❑ Choose **four** of your favourite ones from these examples. Record them on this table. Explain why you chose your collective noun.

Item	Collective noun	Why I chose the collective noun

❑ Can you think of other things you could create collective nouns for?

Find the collections

❑ Look at this wordsearch. Try finding **ten** collective nouns. Write them in the table below. Try to find the things they collect. Write these alongside their collective nouns.

Collective noun	Collects	Collective noun	Collects

z	n	o	t	r	e	e	s	g	c	p	n	s	u	c
w	h	l	p	a	b	u	n	c	h	k	r	a	z	a
h	s	c	h	o	o	l	v	o	e	q	j	b	g	r
a	e	s	n	v	x	a	r	w	s	v	h	e	r	d
l	j	c	l	o	t	h	e	s	t	l	a	e	a	s
e	k	r	a	d	c	p	e	o	p	l	e	s	p	c
s	f	o	r	e	s	t	q	f	x	s	m	w	e	g
t	v	w	n	b	m	o	d	r	a	w	e	r	s	f
k	x	d	e	c	k	p	t	e	t	a	b	p	q	x
a	h	i	w	b	i	r	d	s	y	r	s	u	i	t
f	l	o	c	k	a	n	v	z	o	m	n	f	g	z

Person

Objective
Understand the need for grammatical agreement

Language issues
Pronouns and nouns can be used in the first, second or third person.

The different types of person are indicated by the use of subject pronouns (such as 'I', and 'she') and verbs.

❏ *First person* verbs identify with the speaker or writer, either alone ('I swam') or as part of a group ('we swam').

❏ *Second person* verbs identify with one addressed by the speaker or writer ('You must remember…')

❏ *Third person* verbs identify with a third party or thing who is neither the one addressing nor the one addressed ('He shouted', 'It fell').

Ways of teaching
In children's language use the teaching of person should be oriented towards securing grammatical agreement within the sentences children use. Children need to be aware that some verb forms agree according to the person addressed – 'you were', for example, as opposed to 'you was'.

About the activities
Photocopiable: Choose the right word
There are only certain words that will fit the spaces in these sentences. Children will need to read around the spaces looking at other parts of the sentence that give clues to which word should be used. As children try to find the right word to fit the spaces in the sentences they can try to use a process of elimination. They can look out for the words that do not fit into the spaces and, on this basis, work out which words do.

Photocopiable: Person
As children change the person of these sentences they should be encouraged to use the guidance in the earlier part of the photocopiable page as a way of figuring out their rewordings. The idea of the sentences pointing can be a helpful way of deciding how to reword sentences in the first, second and third person.

Photocopiable: Person in texts
These text extracts both show varying examples of person and also introduce the way in which different types of text use this aspect of grammar in different ways. The use of the first person pronoun and verb is natural in diary-writing, as is the use of the second person for instructions in a recipe. This use of person in the structuring of texts is something children will revisit as they attempt to write a wider range of texts.

Following up
Pass the sentence: Children can try working in threes to say a sentence in the first person ('I found a sweet'), then pass it on. The next speaker has to say the same thing in the second person pointing to the original speaker ('You found a sweet'). The last speaker has to point to the first and say the same thing in the third person ('She found a sweet'). They can try doing this quickly and helping each other with any difficult examples.

Text sorting: Children can look at different extracts from a range of texts to see what person tends to be used. They can look for correspondences between the job done and the person of a text, such as the use of second person in directions.

Choose the right word

❑ Look at these sentences.
Choose a word from the word box that will fit the space in each sentence.

Yesterday Mel and Terry _____ climbing a tree. Mel

_____ climbing fastest. Terry _____ a bit slower

but _____ said,

"We _____ the best climbers."

Mel waved _____ arms and said, "Look at _____ .

I _____ better than _____ ."

Terry said, "Don't say that. It _____ a race."

Mel said, "Yes it _____ and I _____ winning."

Just then _____ foot slipped. _____ grabbed a

branch.

"Careful! _____ nearly fell,"

Terry shouted.

_____ both started to

climb down.

they	you	am
are	isn't	were
	her	you
me	was	
		is
her	she	he
	am	was

❑ Draw a comic strip of the story on the back of this sheet.
Use speech bubbles to show what the characters are saying.

Person

Texts can be written in the first person, the second person or the third person.

First person words are words that point to the writer.
Words like 'I' 'we' 'my' 'our'.

Second person words are words that point to the reader.
Words like 'you' and 'your'.

Third person words are words that point to other things or people.
Words like 'he' 'she' 'it' 'them'.

These sentences are written in the first person. Can you change them to the second person? Can you then change them to the third person?

I kicked the ball. → You kicked the ball. → He kicked the ball.

I played my games.

We ate all our biscuits.

I read this all by myself.

This house is mine.

Can you try the same changes with **six** sentences you have made up?

Person in texts

❏ Look at these snippets of text. Are they written in the first person, second person or third person?

❏ Circle the words that tell you which person the text is written in.

Extract from a recipe
To make an omelette you will need two eggs and some margarine.
First you beat the eggs until the white is mixed with the yolk. Then you melt the margarine in a frying pan. You may need to ask a grown up to help you with this.

Message from librarian to class 4
Message for class 4: Could you bring your library books when you come to the hall? You will be going straight to the library after assembly. Take your book bags from the basket in the classroom and tick yourself off the list by the door.

Experiment
The snails were placed in their tank along with lettuce, chocolate and a piece of bread. They were checked after one hour. Three of the snails were eating the lettuce. None of them were eating the chocolate. None of them were eating the bread.

Extract from newspaper article
Carrie Lewis has fulfilled her ambition. She has been chosen to play for England. Carrie, aged 10, received a letter yesterday saying she had been selected for the England under-11 team. Now she is getting herself ready to travel down to London for training.

Can you take a sentence from each text and change the person?

Sentences making sense

Objective
Develop awareness of longer sentences through
experimenting with the deletion of words
Understand the use of commas in longer sentences

Language issues
In speech and writing some words are more essential
than others. We can précis a text down to essential
words, something writers of notes do all the time. People
who write reminders to themselves scribble the main
words of a thought on a piece of paper (such as 'Key –
Sally Tues' as a reminder to 'Give Sally the key on
Tuesday').

Certain words are essential to meaning; others can be
deleted without losing the meaning of the sentence.
However, these other words tend to help the sentence to
read smoothly. These additional words make the
difference between: 'However, these other words tend to
help the sentence to read smoothly' and 'Other words
help sentence smoothly'. Although the latter example
makes sense, it is not a grammatical sentence.

The use of the comma in sentences indicates a pause
between various items or clauses. In reading, the comma
indicates that the reader pauses before reading on.

Ways of teaching
As children expand the length and vocabulary of the
sentences they use and read, an understanding of the
comma is important. Experimenting with deletion is one
of the ways in which children can explore the
information contained within a sentence and the types of
word that carry it.

About the activities
Photocopiable: Word chopping
Through grasping the meanings of the sentences in this
activity children can decide which words can be
removed. They need to be ruthless. Stress that they are

trying to make the shortest sentence out of the words
available; they must try to discard as much as possible.
This will lead to different results as some decide the
words 'broken beyond repair' are all essential while
others feel it is sufficient to say 'broken'. For this reason
it is best if children work and discuss in pairs.

Photocopiable: Putting words into sentences
This activity builds up given words into a sentence.
Within the given words there are some that will become
the essential words in the sentence. Once they have
written their sentences children could try the word
chopping activity on their own products and see which
words can get the chop. Alternatively they could pass
their examples to a partner and see what word chopping
someone else would perform on their sentences.

Photocopiable: Commas in reading
The use of commas in this exercise is limited to the way
they separate items in a list and separate the clauses in a
sentence. The activity is best done as part of a discussion
with children in which they have the opportunity both to
read aloud and to hear passages from the text read out.

Following up
Telegrams: Children can write messages about events to
imaginary recipients far away. They could write about
their plans for a holiday or a recent event in their family.
Once they have done this they have to try chopping the
message down to old telegram style, keeping the
minimum number of words. They will need some
explanation as to what a telegram was and the way in
which people used to use words sparingly in them.

Sentence strips: Using sentences they have written on
strips of paper, children can cut out the words they think
are essential to the meaning and communication of the
sentence.

Sentences chopped and back again: Working in pairs one
child has to produce a sentence and chop as many words
as they can from it, while retaining the meaning in a way
they can communicate to another. They then hand this
minimal version to their partner who has to rewrite the
original. In a large space like a school hall with two sides
working simultaneously on their sentences and
exchanging edited versions in the middle, this can
provide amusement when the originals are compared
with the 'restoration' job done by a partner.

Word chopping

❑ Work with a partner. Cut out the sentences below. Take turns to read them and say what they are about. Once you have read them, try cutting words out of the strip while keeping a sentence that makes sense.

If the sentence says

Yesterday the little dog was scared by my aunty's motorbike.

we can cut out six words:

and the sentence still makes sense: *The dog was scared.*

On Tuesday we had a big party in the classroom.

The purple monster ate the purple fruit.

The thunder suddenly roared.

Our teachers made a fantastic new treehouse for us.

The little boat sailed down the fast stream.

Your cup of tea that was made half an hour ago is cold.

The big, old, spooky house is very cold.

The classroom ceiling light is completely and totally broken beyond repair.

Putting words into sentences

❏ Put the words in each word bin into a sentence. Use any other words you
need to make the sentence. Make sure you include all the words in each word
bin in one sentence. Make a list of your sentences on a separate sheet of paper.

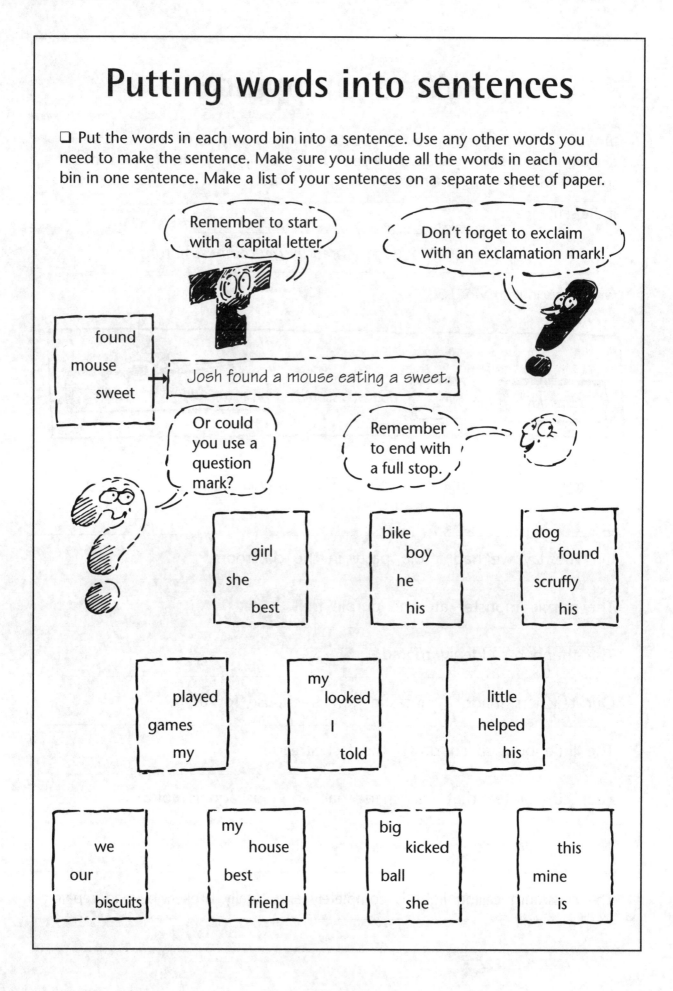

Remember to start
with a capital letter.

Don't forget to exclaim
with an exclamation mark!

found
mouse
sweet

→ Josh found a mouse eating a sweet.

Or could
you use a
question
mark?

Remember
to end with
a full stop.

girl
she
best

bike
boy
he
his

dog
found
scruffy
his

played
games
my

my
looked
I
told

little
helped
his

we
our
biscuits

my
house
best
friend

big
kicked
ball
she

this
mine
is

Scholastic Literacy Skills
Grammar and punctuation

Commas in reading

Two of the main uses of commas are:
❏ to separate items in a list
The dog is short, smelly, scruffy and friendly.
❏ to separate parts of a sentence
The dog, the smelly one, was friendly.

❏ Look at this story:

We bundled our umbrellas out of the taxi.

The train was the last one that day.

We nearly missed the train.
The weather was gloomy, drizzly, cold and wet.
We found a taxi, it nearly drove past us.
The taxi was held up by traffic lights, a level crossing, a diversion, a traffic jam and road works.
The next train, the last one that day, was due to leave at eight o' clock.
It was five minutes to eight.
Then, just as I thought we were too late, we saw the station.
We bundled our bags, coats, umbrellas and the pushchair out of the taxi.
Running like crazy, we dashed across to the platform.
We got to the platform and, as luck would have it, the guard hadn't blown his whistle.
We made it!

The weather was cold.

We saw the station.

The taxi nearly drove past us.

The weather was wet.

We ran like crazy.

We were lucky.

We were held up by a traffic jam.

We were held up by a level crossing.

I thought we were too late.

We went to the platform.

❏ Look for the parts of the story that tell us the things in the boxes.
Draw an arrow from each box to the right part of the story.

The right words

Objective
Use grammatical awareness to decipher new and unfamiliar text

Language issues
'Sally flooggled the tap with a moodle.'
'Sue shouted fragglumly at the squiltish waiter.'
Before you put the book down, be assured the above is gibberish! However, within the gibberish most competent users of English will be able to recognize
- what Sally did with the tap
- what Sally used for the task
- the manner in which Sue shouted
- what the waiter was like.

The nonsense words used in these sentences occupied spaces we can identify as, for example, the place a verb would go. They also had endings that language users recognize as belonging to regular parts of speech.

As sentences are combined there are spaces within them that are understood as the place for a particular type of word. 'With a...' sets up the sentence to feature a noun. The noun that is selected may be nonsense but as children learn to read, encountering new and unfamiliar words, this understanding of what sort of word they can expect in a particular space is an essential part of their decoding skills.

Ways of teaching
This unit looks at the way in which spaces in sentences are likely to accommodate certain word types. An understanding of grammar can make it more specific whether a space is suited to, for example, a plural noun or particular types of pronoun.

About the activities
Photocopiable: Sentences to change
As children alter these sentences they will be using their understanding of how the words should fit together. Once they have selected the words they will change, they can discuss the reasons for making their chosen alterations.

Photocopiable: Choose and place the words
The fitting of the words in this cloze activity into the right spaces can involve trial and error. Children can try various combinations until they find the one that works best.

Photocopiable: Missing words
Once children have completed the selection of words in this activity they could compare their lists with a partner and see what similarities and differences there are in their chosen words.

Following up
Nonsense Words: As with the opening of the 'Language issues' section, children can try to look at sentences with nonsense words and consider what type of words they could be. If, for example, the missing word is an adjective they can consider what noun it is describing, whether it sounds complementary, and so on.

Missing word: Children can look at a simple sentence with a word missing, such as 'The ____ climbed the tree' and list possible words for the missing word. They can begin with the more obvious ('monkey', 'children') and then expand to the less likely ('shopping trolley'). Point out that, outlandish though such suggestions may be, they can provide entertaining images and also are in keeping with the type of word selected for the space in the sentence.

Likelihood: Working from a list of possible words to fill a space in a particular sentence, as devised in the above activity, children can then review the suggestions and give them marks out of ten for how likely they are. So in the above example 'monkey' gets a high score and 'shopping trolley' a low one.

Sentences to change

❑ Look at these sentences. Which word is the correct one? Discuss them with a partner. Can you write them using the correct word?

This is/am the park. _____

My best friend were/was on the climbing frame. _____

We was/were going on the swings. _____

I is/am going home. _____

We is/are playing in the park. _____

Two of my friends was/were on the see saw. _____

Me/I like the slide. _____

You/He are welcome to join us. _____

We is/are going back again tomorrow. _____

Choose and place the words

Each of these sentences has some words missing. The words are underneath the sentences. Can you rebuild the sentence? Can you choose the right word for the right space?

Izzy _____ the _____ .
window/opened

The _____ landed on the _____ .
spaceship/planet

_____ hamster _____ a bit smelly.
our/is

On _____ _____ watched _____ video.
we/Thursday/the

I _____ in _____ friend's _____ .
garden/played/my

Marcus _____ to the _____ on the _____ .
music/radio/danced

I can see the _____ _____ on the river.
boat/little

We went to _____ airport _____ saw _____ planes.
the/some/and

When _____ go swimming _____ take_____ towel.
I/we/my

I _____ to _____ my _____ .
teeth/forgot/clean

Sara fell off _____ bike and _____ helped_____ .
my/her/we

Scholastic Literacy Skills
Grammar and punctuation

Missing words

❑ Look at the spaces in the sentences. Try thinking of **three** different words that could fit in each space. Write all three in each box.

The [_____] fell off the wall.

A [_____] climbed a [_____].

The [_____] monster ate the flowers.

My [_____] is in my house.

[_____] hand has got five fingers.

The girl [_____] the ball.

We can [_____] a [_____].

❑ Can you see anything each of the sets of three words you chose have in common?

Pronouns

Contents of Term 3a

This half-term

Pronouns are introduced and investigated throughout this half-term's units. Their uses in text are looked at and there is a revision of the concept of first, second and third person.

Poster notes

The pronouns

This poster presents the various words that can function as personal pronouns. They are organized into rows of singular and plural pronouns. Children may note the way in which some pronouns retain a particular form within a variety of columns. The poster provides an opportunity for children to think of sentences in which they would use particular pronouns.

Person

The same pronouns are organized into first, second and third person pronouns. Children could try figuring out which ones are singular and which are plural.

The pronouns

I	me	my	mine	myself
you	you	your	yours	yourself
he	him	his	his	himself
she	her	her	hers	herself
we	us	our	ours	ourselves
they	them	their	theirs	themselves

Person

First person
I
me
my
mine
myself
we
us
our
ours
ourselves

Second person
you
your
yours
yourself
yourselves

Third person
he
him
his
himself
she
her
hers
herself
they
them
their
theirs
themselves

Pronouns and noun phrases

Objective
Identify pronouns

Language issues
Pronouns are words that are substituted for nouns or noun phrases. In the sentence 'Joe gave the cake to Samia' the noun 'Joe' can be substituted for the pronoun 'he' to make 'He gave the cake to Samia'. The other nouns, the cake and Samia, can also be substituted to make 'He gave it to her'.

Pronouns are relatively anonymous words. In the above example Joe may be a particular person but 'He' could refer to any one of half the population. Similarly 'the cake' is more definite than 'it'. When pronouns are used they tend to require a shared understanding of whom or what they refer to.

Pronouns stand in for nouns but, unlike nouns, they cannot be modified by adjectives. So whereas the usage 'He gave the delicious cake to her' is straightforward, the sentence 'He gave the delicious it to her' isn't. The only way of using an adjective here would be to use the construction 'the … one', as in 'the delicious one' – but this implies a further meaning that there is 'one' that *isn't* delicious.

Ways of teaching
Children need to grasp a basic understanding of a pronoun as one of a general and relatively small family of words that can be substituted for a noun. Once they have seen a list of the words that can perform this function (on the photocopiable page 'Who is "you"?') they will often begin to find examples for themselves in texts they are reading.

About the activities
Photocopiable: Who is 'you'?
This activity takes children through a text artificially inflated with pronouns. In doing this it gives children an idea of the way such words function. One way of reading the text is for children to imagine the pronouns as words that are pointing and, as they read them, to ask 'Who am I pointing at as I say this word?' The idea of pointing as they say 'we' or 'that' should enhance the way the pronouns work in this text.

Photocopiable: Pronouns in action
As children undertake this activity they need a variety of texts. The teacher may find it useful to skim read the texts beforehand to check which pronouns they contain. Children may also use texts they bring from home in which they have noticed pronouns.

Photocopiable: Awkward sentences
As children read the sentences in this activity they are asked to alter the ones that sound 'awkward'. This may provide an opportunity to discuss the redrafting or editing process that takes place in the production of texts and ask children to imagine they are undertaking this task.

Following up
Exhaustive list: The pronoun family is not vast. Children may be able to compile the exhaustive list. As they read through various texts they can put forward examples they find of words that may be pronouns. The class can consider whether or not they are and, if so, add them to the list.

Newspaper circling: Children can work in threes and fours looking through a copy of a newspaper and circling all the words they think may be pronouns. They may be able to handle the task of applying the question 'If this word is a pronoun, what noun does it stand in for?'

Customize 'you': Once they have tried the 'Who is "you"?' photocopiable activity, children can try to produce their own example using a photocopied text. They can isolate the pronouns and write, in the margins, the questions the reader needs to answer in order to understand the pronoun being used.

Who is 'you'?

❑ Look at the story below. In it there are words like:

you	yourself	we	us	our
he	him	they	their	
she		them	those	that
it				

They refer to someone or something. They stand in for a noun (the name of something). Words that stand in for someone or something are called **pronouns**.

Who or what does each of the pronouns in the story refer to? The pronouns are the words shown in bold type:

Natasha took Monty her dog for **their** afternoon walk.
He didn't like being on **his** lead so he pulled and pulled
at **it**. Natasha let **him** lead the way. As **they** walked **she**
chatted to herself.
"Where are **you** taking **us** ?" she asked Monty.
They came to the park.
"We can stop here if you like," she said. "**We** don't need
to be home for **our** tea yet."
She found a stick and threw **it**.
"Can you chase **that**?" she said. Monty found it.
Then she threw two sticks. "O.K." she shouted, "Chase
those."
She threw **them** as far as she could. **They** landed up in a
tree!
"Fetch them **yourself**," Monty growled.

Pronouns in action

❑ Look in some texts. You could look in picture books, a newspaper, an advert, a letter… any texts you choose.

❑ Find some of these pronouns in your texts:

I   me   my   mine   myself   you   yours   yourself   he   him   his   himself
she   her   hers   herself   we   us   our   ours   ourselves   they   them
their   theirs   it   its   itself   this   these   that   those

❑ Write the pronouns in the pronoun column below.
Next to the pronoun write the person or thing it stands in for.

Pronoun	What the pronoun stands in for (the noun)

Awkward sentences

Some of the nouns in these sentences don't need to be there.

> *Dave found (Dave's) coat.*

They could be taken away:

> *Dave found ~~(Dave's)~~ coat.*

Pronouns could be put in their place:

> *Dave found his coat.*

❑ Replace the circled nouns with pronouns. Write them above each of the circled words.

Here are some pronouns you could use:

his	it	her	I	she	him	us
them	they	his	our	me		
he	you		my	we	their	

After school

Dave forgot (Dave's) coat.

Carrie bought an apple and ate (the apple).

Carrie asked (Carrie's) mum, "Can (Carrie) have an ice cream?"

Mel got (Mel's) football then (Mel) went out to play.

Dave's teacher told (Dave) that (Dave) had forgotten (Dave's) coat.

Mel told Carrie, "(Carrie) can borrow (Mel's) pencil."

Joe and Rose asked (Joe and Rose's) mum, "Can (Joe and Rose) play outside?"

Joe and Rose told Carrie, "(Carrie) can play with (Joe and Rose) at (Joe and Rose's) house."

Rose stood on (Rose's) head and said, "Look at (Rose)."

Frank called for Joe and Rose and (Frank) asked (Joe and Rose) if (Joe and Rose) wanted to play at (Frank's) house.

PHOTOCOPIABLE

Pronouns take their place

Objective
Substitute pronouns for nouns

Language issues
Pronouns are often used to make sentences more readable. A sentence like 'Leah rode Leah's bike to Leah's house' is an oddity. The form 'Leah rode her bike to her house' is tidier.

The link between the pronoun and the noun for which it stands is called reference. If the pronoun refers to a noun that follows it in a text (for example 'Because he wasn't looking, Sam tripped up'), this is called a *cataphoric* reference. If the pronoun stands for a noun that has already occurred in a text (for example 'Sam said he was tired') it is called *anaphoric* reference. To avoid ambiguity the pronoun needs clear referential relationship with a noun.

Ways of teaching
As children begin to reflect upon pronouns they need to focus upon their own use of this type of word. They can begin to check in their own writing for the clarity with which they use pronouns.

About the activities
Photocopiable: Change the sentence
As children substitute pronouns for noun phrases the results will vary. A sentence like 'Don't eat the cakes' could be changed to 'Don't eat them' or 'Don't eat those'. It may be interesting to look at the pronoun children use for 'My best friend…' Will they use 'he' or 'she'? What guided their choice?

Photocopiable: What do they refer to?
This missing word activity works on the referential function of pronouns. To find the appropriate word children will need to consider what the pronouns actually refer to.

Photocopiable: Choose the pronoun
As children consider their options for the pronoun they could select for the sentences on this photocopiable page, there will be discussion. Some of the children may have encountered younger children who would say 'Me went to the beach'. In certain dialects 'Us teacher' as opposed to 'Our teacher' could be used. The various possibilities can provide some insights into the varied uses of pronouns and their commonly accepted usage.

Following up
Pronoun links: Children can look for pronouns in a text such as a newspaper article, and circle examples. They can then try to find the noun the pronoun stands in for, in the same text. They can circle the noun and link it to the pronoun.

Reference: Children can look at the position of pronouns in relation to their nouns. They can see if the pronoun precedes or follows the noun. Obscure though they may be, terms like 'anaphoric' and 'cataphoric' can go down well with children.

Change the sentence

❑ Look at these sentences. Find one word in the word box that can stand in for the phrase underlined. Change them and write them in the space underneath.

I saw <u>the little boy</u> fall off his skateboard.
I saw him fall off his skateboard.

her	them	he
this	us	him
these		she
those		it
		we

Julie played on <u>her new roller skates</u>.

_____

Don't eat <u>the cakes</u>.

_____

Can Warren play with <u>the computer games</u>?

_____

Did you find <u>the lost key</u>?

_____

The teacher told <u>Leila and me</u> we could use <u>the cricket bat</u>.

_____

The boy gave <u>his little sister</u> a sweet.

_____

The teacher said, "Give me <u>the sweets</u>!"

_____

Mum couldn't get <u>the television</u> to work.

_____

<u>Shaun</u> said <u>Josh and I</u> could have a go on <u>his bike</u>.

_____

<u>My best friend</u> can do a magic trick.

_____

❑ Turn over this sheet and list the pronouns you used and the phrases they stood in for.

What do they refer to?

❑ Look at the gaps in the sentences below. Find a word in the pronoun box that fits in each gap.

hers that mine
we you
I them him they
us
she he
our it himself

The animals were at a party. _____ were bored. Monkey wanted to cheer

_____ up. She found a tree stump and jumped on_____ .

She shouted to the animals "Hey _____ lot – look at me."

She did a funny dance. _____ bopped and jived. The animals laughed so

loudly _____ gave themselves tummy aches.

The camel was not pleased. _____ was so jealous.

When the monkey was finished he clambered onto the tree stump.

"If she can do it so can _____," he thought. He did a dance.

"I bet _____ is better than _____ ," he said to _____ .

The animals thought camel was awful. They shouted " _____ is rubbish.

What do you take_____ for?_____ don't want any old dancing.

Bring back _____ friend the monkey."

They sent _____ packing.

A fable by *Aesop*

Choose the pronoun

❑ Look at the sentences below. There are three possible pronouns in each one. Rewrite the sentences, choosing the pronoun that suits the sentence.

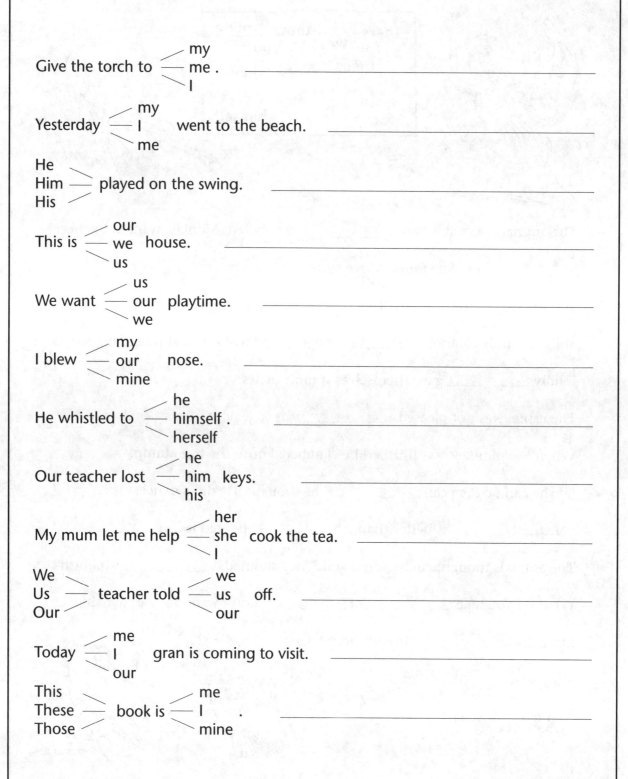

Give the torch to — my / me . / I _____

Yesterday — my / I / me went to the beach. _____

He / Him / His played on the swing. _____

This is — our / we / us house. _____

We want — us / our / we playtime. _____

I blew — my / our / mine nose. _____

He whistled to — he / himself / herself . _____

Our teacher lost — he / him / his keys. _____

My mum let me help — her / she / I cook the tea. _____

We / Us / Our teacher told — we / us / our off. _____

Today — me / I / our gran is coming to visit. _____

This / These / Those book is — me / I / mine . _____

Two types of pronoun

Objective
Distinguish personal and possessive pronouns

Language issues
There are various types of pronoun. *Personal pronouns* replace the names of people or things, for example 'I', 'me', 'they'. *Possessive pronouns*, self-evidently, indicate possession of something, such as 'mine', 'his', 'theirs'. They refer to something in the same context as the pronoun that can be identified as a possession. In the sentence 'John took my book', the use of a possessive pronoun would result in 'John took mine'.

Note that the possessive words used attributively (that is to say, *before* the noun), are possessive adjectives, or possessive determiners, since they modify the noun. This category includes words such as 'my', 'your', 'his', 'her' and so on.

Ways of teaching
The distinction made between these types of pronoun can provide a way of expanding children's awareness of the pronouns they encounter. It provides two separate ways of thinking about, and looking for, pronouns. Where a possessive pronoun is used they will usually be able to identify the thing that is possessed.

About the activities
Photocopiable: Two types of pronoun
As an introduction to the distinction between personal and possessive pronouns, this activity uses simple sentences and asks children to categorize the pronouns within them.

Photocopiable: Matching personal and possessive
The mixing of personal and possessive pronouns in this activity leads children to try matching up sentences in which the two types of pronoun correspond. The emphasis in this activity should be upon children saying the sentences aloud to see if the result sounds right.

Photocopiable: Possessives
Through reflecting on the different people referred to in this activity children should fall back on the possessive pronouns and adjectives they know to find the right word to begin each of the sentences. Again, the gender of the person will decide the correct pronoun.

Following up
Possessive listings: Using the 'Possessives' photocopiable as a starting point children can write short paragraphs about people, including individuals and groups. They could draw on themselves, their group of friends, an older brother or sister as a starting point. Once they have chosen their person or persons they write a few sentences about them, using the appropriate pronouns.

Matching: Children can write the name of a person or group of people on one card and a sentence about them on another. In the sentence they can try using a personal or possessive pronoun. They can then try producing two different cards, choosing whoever they wish provided their choice leads them to use different pronouns.

Two types of pronoun

There are different types of pronoun.
Two of the different types of pronoun are

> **personal pronouns:**
> Pronouns that stand in place of a
> person or thing (me, I, you, it)

and

> **possessive pronouns:**
> Pronouns that show someone owns
> something (my, mine, yours, ours).

❑ Look at the sentences below. Sort them into two groups:
- sentences with possessive pronouns
- sentences with personal pronouns.

Sam is my friend.

I like sweets.

Sian found her shoe.

You are reading.

He fell in the puddle.

The red pencil is mine.

We can go to the park.

My tooth is hurting.

They are going on holiday.

We can go out to play.

Our teacher is loud.

These sweets are all yours.

Matching personal and possessive

❑ Cut out the strips below.

Try matching the strips on one side of the page with the strips on the other side of the page. The result will be two sentences that fit together.

This bike belongs to me.

This book belongs to you.

That coat belongs to him.

This football belongs to her.

This house belongs to them.

This television belongs to us.

These stickers belong to me.

These crayons belong to you.

These sandwiches belong to him.

These shoes belong to her.

These sweets belong to them.

These flowers belong to us.

They are theirs.

It is his.

They are hers.

They are ours.

They are mine.

They are his.

It is hers.

It is ours.

It is yours.

It is my mine.

They are yours.

It is theirs.

❑ Stick the matching sentences on a separate sheet of paper.

Possessives

❑ Look at the sentences below. Think about the people referred to in each sentence. Complete the sentence, filling in the possessive pronoun and the end of the sentence.

About me.

<u>My</u> task is <u>finding missing words.</u>

About my friend.

—— name is ————————.

About my school.

—— classrooms are ————

————————.

About our teachers.

—— staff room is ————

————————.

About me and my friend.

—— favourite game is ————

————.

About my bedroom.

—— floor is ————————.

About our headteacher.

—— favourite day of the week is

————————.

About me.

—— favourite pop song is ————

————————.

❑ Try some possessive sentences of your own about other people. It could be people in your family or people in your street.

Different types of pronoun

Objective
Distinguish first, second and third person pronouns

Language issues
Pronouns can be written in the first, second or third person.

❑ *First person* pronouns identify with the speaker or writer, either alone ('I swam') or as part of a group ('we swam').

❑ *Second person* pronouns identify with one addressed by the speaking or writing ('You must remember…')

❑ *Third person* pronouns identify with a third party or thing who is neither the one addressing nor the one addressed ('He shouted', 'It fell').

Ways of teaching
An understanding of first, second and third person can be an important factor in children's writing development. As children widen the variety of texts they produce through work on the style and language of explanatory and persuasive texts, they can look at the way certain texts are couched in the first, second or third person. A persuasive text may use the second person ('You should buy this…') whereas a recount of a personal experience will adopt the first person ('I went to school and I…').

About the activities
Photocopiable: Person
As with the understanding of what a pronoun stands in for, the initial approach to person can be assisted by pointing. As they read the sentences in this activity the children can imagine themselves saying them to another person (the second person) and pointing at the person to whom the pronoun refers. If they point to themselves the sentence uses the first person. If they point to the listener it uses the second. If they point outside the conversation to something else, the pronoun is in the third person.

Photocopiable: Ways of looking at pronouns
Once they have applied the two criteria to the examples in the photocopiable children could try this activity using other sentences from various texts.

Photocopiable: Pronouns at play
This reading activity may be used in shared or guided reading. Once children have read through the script they should try looking at the various types of pronoun used in the text.

Following up
Taping: Children could tape classroom conversation. They could then listen to the tape and consider whether the pronouns used are first, second or third person. They could keep a tally of the most common usage in the conversation.

I, you, he texts: Children could try writing sentences in each person. Once they have completed a set of examples they could look at them to see what text they could imagine such sentences featuring in. What text, for example, would be couched in the second person?

Person

First person words are words that point to the writer – It's how you write if you are writing about yourself.

Second person words are words that point to the reader – It's how you write if you are writing about your reader.

Third person words are words that point to other things or people – It's how you write if you are writing about someone or something else.

❑ Cut out these sentences. Say them aloud. Sort them into sentences written in the first person, the second person and the third person. Stick them in their three groups on a separate sheet of paper.

Six o' clock is time for them to have their tea.

You ate all your dinner.

They went shopping.

Did you finish the story?

The bike is mine.

You found the pencil.

At playtime I saw my sister.

I ate all my dinner.

We went shopping.

Did he finish the story?

The bike is hers.

At playtime you saw your sister.

Did we finish the story?

You went shopping.

They found the pencil.

The bike is yours.

Six o' clock is time for you to have your tea.

I had chips for tea.

They had chips for their tea.

She ate all her dinner.

Six o' clock is time for me to have my tea.

You had chips for tea.

At playtime he saw his sister.

We found the pencil.

Ways of looking at pronouns

❑ Look at the pronouns used in each of the text extracts below.
Are they personal pronouns or possessive pronouns? Are they first person,
second person or third person pronouns?

I switched on the television.

Personal or possessive?

First person, second person or third person?

My mum likes chocolate.

Personal or possessive?

First person, second person or third person?

Our classroom is tidy.

Personal or possessive?

First person, second person or third person?

Rafi played on his skateboard.

Personal or possessive?

First person, second person or third person?

My sister tidied her room.

Personal or possessive?

First person, second person or third person?

You are smiling.

Personal or possessive?

First person, second person or third person?

Your shirt is ripped.

Personal or possessive?

First person, second person or third person?

The children sang their song.

Personal or possessive?

First person, second person or third person?

Pronouns at play

❏ Act out this play with some friends.

Cast:
Hare
Tortoise
Fox

Fox: This is a story of two animals and how they decided who was the fastest.

(Hare is sitting with Fox. Tortoise comes past.)

Hare: Hello Tortoise

Tortoise: Hello Hare. Hello Fox.

Hare: Oh dear, you are so slow.

Tortoise: Am I?

Hare: She is, isn't she, Fox?

Fox: Leave her alone, Hare.

Tortoise: O.K. Why don't we have a race? The winner will get a medal.

Hare: A race! With you! Ha! I will easily win.

Tortoise: We shall see. Fox, could you start us off?

Fox: Alright. Are you ready? Steady? Go?

(Hare runs far into the lead.)

Hare: Look at me go. The medal will be mine!

Fox: Hurry up Tortoise. Oh dear, she is sure to lose

Tortoise: Don't worry about me. I know what I'm doing.

(Hare is well in the lead.)

Hare: Where is she? I can't even see her. I think I'll have a rest.

(Falls asleep. Tortoise comes past.)

Tortoise: Just as I thought. He is fast asleep. Shhh, don't want to wake him.

(Fox stands at the finishing line.)

Fox: Come on tortoise. This is your chance to win.

(Hare wakes up. Sees Tortoise crossing line.)

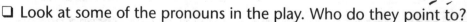

Hare: She beat me!

❏ Look at some of the pronouns in the play. Who do they point to?
❏ Read the play again. Each time you come to a pronoun stop and point to the character it refers to.

Pronouns in texts

Objective
Investigate the use of pronouns

Language issues
Pronouns can be ambiguous words. For example, a note sent by a member of the public to the local council read: 'Our kitchen floor is very damp. We have two children and would like a third. Could you please send someone round to do something about it?' That final 'it' is full of ambiguity.

The clear use of pronouns is a stylistic feature that needs to be considered. Yet the ambiguity can be used to full effect, whether it be in the Thomas Hardy poem in this unit or in a joke like the one used throughout the film *Airplane*:

Passenger: Hostess, take me to the cockpit!
Hostess: What is it?
Passenger: It's a little room at the front of the plane with controls and things, but that's not important right now.

Ways of teaching
Through this unit children should grasp the potential in investigating the use of the pronoun. They should also get some idea of the poetic use of this type of word as well as its common use in conversation.

About the activities
Photocopiable: 'Waiting Both'
This activity draws out the poetic use of pronouns to their full effect. As children read the poem they can consider the effect of the use of pronouns as opposed to more specific names.

Photocopiable: Comic pronouns
As with many comic stories children will find, as they read this text, that an understanding of the pronouns depends on an appreciation of what they are referring to. In some cases this will rely on the picture rather than the text. So the 'there' in 'Can we go in there?' is only understood through reference to the illustration.

Photocopiable: Pronoun talk
As children record and investigate their use of pronouns they can compare their findings with others in the class. They could also swap tapes and listen to the conversations others have taped.

Following up
Poetry: Other poems, such as Stevie Smith's 'Not waving but drowning' feature consciously ambiguous uses of pronouns. Children could try their own examples.

Eerie openings: Stories can often use pronouns to provide an eerie opening, for example, 'He was late. He ran through the streets. What if they got there before him?' Children could try creating their own mysterious story openings in the same vein.

'Waiting Both'

❏ Look at this poem.

A star looks down at me,
And says: 'Here I am and you
Stand each in our degree:
What do you mean to do,-
    Mean to do?'

I say: 'For all I know,
Wait, and let Time go by
Till my change comes.'-'Just so',
The Star says: 'So mean I:-
    So mean I.'

Thomas Hardy

❏ Find the pronouns in the poem.
❏ Look at the words taken from the poem in the boxes below. What do you think about these lines?

A star looks down at me,	I think...

'Here I am and you Stand each in our degree:	I think...

What do you mean to do, - Mean to do?'	I think...

'Wait, and let Time go by Till my change comes.'	I think...

The Star says: 'So mean I:- So mean I.'	I think...

Comic pronouns

❑ Look at this story. Find the pronouns in the story and circle them.

❑ Look back at the pronouns. Which person or thing did they refer to?

Pronoun talk

❑ Tape a five-minute conversation with two friends on this subject:
"Things people do at playtime".

❑ Listen to it again. Write down some of the pronouns used in the discussion.
In the box alongside, record who the pronouns referred to.

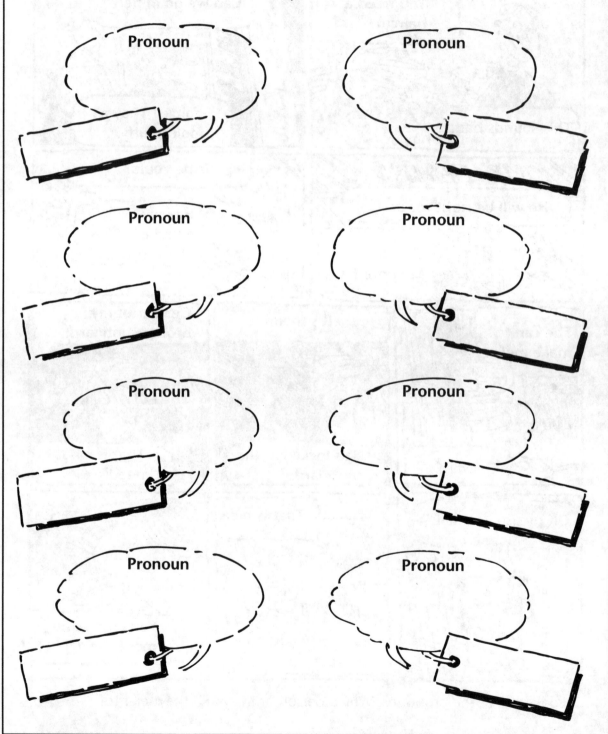

Conjunctions and speech marks

Contents of Term 3b

Unit 1: Use awareness of grammar to decipher new and unfamiliar words
Deciphering words

Unit 2: Use speech marks and other dialogue punctuation
Speech marks

Unit 3: Use a wider range of conjunctions in extending sentences
Conjunctions

Unit 4: Investigate how words and phrases signal time
Time words

Unit 5: Use commas to mark grammatical boundaries in sentences
Sentences working together

This half-term

The main emphasis is upon conjunctions, looking at the different functions that they perform. There is also a unit examining speech marks (inverted commas) and one that revisits the way in which grammar supports the deciphering of words.

The material on conjunctions aims to widen the range of words that children can draw on. As they undertake these units children should be encouraged to try to extend the range of conjunctions used in their day-to-day written work.

Poster notes

Conjunctions at work
The various tasks conjunctions can perform are presented on this poster. The four categories can provide a way of children organizing their learning and investigating of examples of this word class.

Temporal conjunctions
This poster will particularly support work in Unit 4. It provides a range of temporal conjunctions. These can be particularly useful to children involved in writing narrative text, whether it be a story or their own diaries. The different types of temporal conjunction can suggest ways of organizing sentences.

Conjunctions at work

Conjunctions can:

add one thing to another:
eg, I like rain and I like snow.

oppose one thing against another
eg, I like rain but my friend hates it.

show how one thing is caused by another
eg, I like snow because it looks great.

show how one thing is linked to the time of another
eg, We put on warm clothes then we went out in the snow.

Temporal conjunctions

Deciphering words

Objective
Use awareness of grammar to decipher new and unfamiliar words

Language issues
An awareness of grammar can enable readers and listeners to account for words they do not hear clearly or do not understand, as well as words they find new and unfamiliar in reading. As the reader or listener takes in the content of a sentence there are only certain types of word that can possibly fill certain spaces in the sentence. The sentence is combined into a whole and, within its various spaces, certain words are selected as the verbs to describe the action or the noun to name the object. Because of this, language users are able to predict which word will follow and guess at the meaning of obscure words. Other sources of information such as the overall meaning of the text contribute to this collecting together of various cues.

Ways of teaching
In this unit the activities work on the way in which children should be beginning to guess the word that will fill a particular space. However, the important aspect of this unit is that, as the children try and guess words, there should also be some discussion about the *type* of word that would fill a particular space. This may involve the teacher in suggesting words that could <u>not fill</u> a particular space and allowing children to explain why the teacher cannot be right.

About the activities
Photocopiable: Possible words
This activity causes children to fill a number of very different spaces in a sentence. In doing this they need to try and turn the words on the page into something that sounds credible. As they discuss the spaces they will become aware of the fact that a different type of word is required for each gap in the sentence.

Photocopiable: Rebuild the story
By rebuilding the sentences in this photocopiable children will deploy an awareness of word order and how sentences are structured. They will, for example, need to use their awareness that "'Stop!'" can come before or after 'I shouted', but not between these words.

Photocopiable: Break the code
The code in this activity needs to be broken. Some of the more obvious words in the text should give the children the way into finding some of the letter/number correspondences in the code. Once they have done this it will give them more cues to help decipher some of the other words. Again, in doing this, they will be drawing on an understanding of the type of word that could fill each space.

To break the code, split the alphabet in two and number each half in reverse, ie, m–a = 1–13; z–n = 14–26. The missing words in the story are: upon, bears, hot, walk, forest, girl, hungry, opened, inside, very, quiet. 'Try this code' reads: **Quiz**. Can you read this? What is your name? **25.3**

Following up
Own reading: Children can start thinking about the grammatical nature of words they struggle with in their own reading. In particular they can look out for words that appear to do the job of a noun or an adjective and clues that show a word is a plural.

Jigsaw sentences: Working in twos and threes, children can write a sentence out on a strip of card, cut up the individual words and try rebuilding the sentence. This should prove simple enough that they add another sentence. Then another. Each time a cut up sentence is added they have to jumble and rebuild the whole thing. After about the seventh sentence it gets to be a real struggle.

Possible words

❑ Look at these sentences. Suggest words that could fill the gaps.

I wore _____ clothes because I was painting.

The _____ horse _____ over the gate.

The _____ girl _____ the chips.

The room was _____ so we turned on the _____ .

The _____ robber stole the _____ .

We stopped the car _____ because the traffic light was _____ .

He _____ off the _____ wall and hurt his foot.

The man _____ for his change and _____ into the bus.

The pirate found _____ treasure and _____ it.

The _____ parrot said a _____ poem.

My _____ made some _____ cakes.

My _____ sister _____ the ball through the _____ .

A _____ stole my _____ .

❑ Compare with your friends to see if they have written different words in any of the spaces.

Rebuild the story

Each of these boxes contains a jumbled up sentence from a story. Can you rebuild the sentences? Once you have done that can you arrange the sentences to make the story?

driver	bus	The	stopped.

mum	off	bus.	My	the	got.

my	I	bus	was	with	mum.	the	on

shouted	"Stop!"	I

me	stopped	let	driver	and	The	off.

said	"Sorry."	He

to	drive	He	away.	about	was

started	bus	He	again.	the

didn't	me.	The	driver	see

to	bus	We	stop.	came	our

Break the code

Some of these words are written in a code. Can you work out the code by finding out the some of the words? These should start you off working out what letter each number stands for.

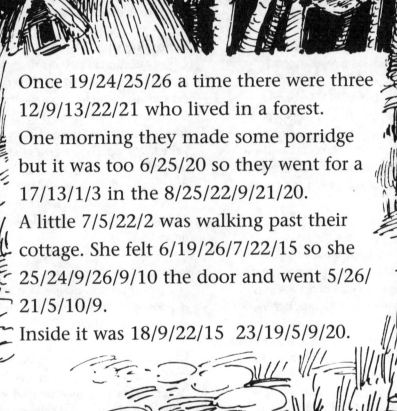

Once 19/24/25/26 a time there were three 12/9/13/22/21 who lived in a forest.

One morning they made some porridge but it was too 6/25/20 so they went for a 17/13/1/3 in the 8/25/22/9/21/20.

A little 7/5/22/2 was walking past their cottage. She felt 6/19/26/7/22/15 so she 25/24/9/26/9/10 the door and went 5/26/21/5/10/9.

Inside it was 18/9/22/15 23/19/5/9/20.

❏ Try this code:

23/19/5/14

11/13/26	15/25/19	22/9/13/10	20/6/5/21?

17/6/13/20	5/21	15/25/19/22	26/13/1/9?

Speech marks

Objective
Use speech marks and other dialogue punctuation

Language issues
Speech marks are used to demarcate the words that were actually spoken in a sentence. In a sentence like 'Mum said, "Tidy up"' the speech marks enclose the words Mum actually said.

Lines of speech can be separated from the words denoting who is speaking in three ways:

❑ The speech can come after the other words:
Mum said, "Can you lot go and tidy your room?"
❑ or before them:
"Can you lot go and tidy your room?" Mum said.
❑ Or the speech can be separated by other words:
"Can you lot go," Mum said, "and tidy your room."

In each of these, the speech marks enclose the actual words said. Commas are also used to mark the gap between a set of words that are spoken and other words.

Ways of teaching
The emphasis in this unit is upon the use of speech marks, though the use of commas in such sentences can also be pointed out. The main idea to get across is the way in which speech marks enclose words that were actually said. This idea can be communicated by envisaging the speech marks as being like a bubble that has been rubbed out leaving the marks behind (see 'Temporal conjunctions' poster).

About the activities
Photocopiable: Marking out speech
As they read the poem 'Overheard on a Saltmarsh' children can try figuring out which of the two speakers is saying the individual lines. This activity can act as a prelude to other reading activities. The piece can be read by two groups taking the parts of the two characters, or the teacher can read one part and the children respond with the other.

Photocopiable: Speech marks
By remodelling the scripted passage as dialogue children get experience of trying a range of words to describe the act of speaking.

Photocopiable: Speech marks 2
As they try to demarcate the words in the sentences on the photocopiable, children will need to figure out which words were actually spoken.

Following up
Carpet talk: During class discussions the teacher can explain to the class that, over the coming week, they are occasionally going to stop a speaker after they have said something and ask the class to figure out how that act of speaking would be recorded in an account of the event written later on. For the next week, every so often, after a child has said something like 'Can I take the register downstairs?' the teacher will stop the class and ask them to model the event as a sentence on the board (for example, 'Fozia asked, "Can I take the register downstairs?"')

Dialogue: Children can find passages in novels in which a group of characters are speaking and try acting out the passage, each taking a role and saying aloud the words ascribed to that character.

Ways of saying: Children can think of as many different ways of saying something as they can. Examples could include 'shrieking', 'sneering' and so on. They can try speaking in this way and deciding which words they would use to denote that manner of speaking.

Marking out speech

There are two speakers in this poem – a nymph and a goblin.
❏ Read the poem carefully.

Overheard on a Saltmarsh

Nymph, nymph, what are your beads?
Green glass, goblin. Why do you stare at them?
Give them me.
> No.
Give them me. Give them me.
> No.
Then I will howl all night in the reeds,
Lie in the mud and howl for them.

Goblin, why do you love them so?

They are better than stars or water,
Better than voices of winds that sing,
Better than any man's fair daughter,
Your green glass beads on a silver ring.

Hush, I stole them out of the moon.

Give my your beads, I desire them.
> No.
I will howl in a deep lagoon
For your green glass beads, I love them so.
Give them me. Give them me.
> No.

Harold Monro

Can you work out which lines the goblin is saying? Can you work out which lines
the nymph is saying?
❏ Shade over the nymph's lines in one colour and the goblin's lines in another.

Speech marks

❏ Look at the conversation below.

Lou's voice

Wake up. It's time for school.

You have to go to school.

You have to go!

You still have to get up for school.

For a very good reason.

You're the headteacher.

Sam's voice

I don't want to go to school.

But all the children hate me.

But all the teachers hate me.

Why do I have to get up for school?

What is it?

❏ Turn over this sheet and rewrite the conversation as a passage with speech. A start has been made for you here.

"Wake up. It's time for school," said Lou.
"I don't want to go to school," grumbled Sam.

Speech words to help you
said   called   grumbled
shouted   mumbled
yelled   moaned

Speech marks 2

These lines have lost their speech marks. Can you rewrite them putting the speech marks in? Change letters that should be capitals and add any other missing punctuation. The final example is much more difficult. Write it out correctly on the back of this sheet.

quick said sam hide the map

help me clean up this mess josh said

hey you the teacher shouted where are you going

can I tidy the art corner the boy asked the teacher

my sock is smellier than yours joe said to sam no it isn't sam replied

boo shouted the girl eek screamed her mum oh you gave me a fright

go away said the scarecrow you can't make us the birds replied can't I he shouted

give us a sweet leah snapped no replied josh ask politely o.k. leah said please give us a sweet that's better said josh

Conjunctions

Objective
Use a wider range of conjunctions in extending sentences

Language issues
Sentences can be simple, for example, 'Joe made tea'. The simple sentence can be added to in a number of ways.

Conjunctions are words used to link material within texts and sentences. Conjunctions are used to join together ('conjoin') two words, phrases or sentences. The word 'and' is the most common conjunction, joining words: 'Joe made tea and coffee and juice' or phrases: 'Joe made hot, sweet tea and much needed coffee and his mum's home made recipe for orange juice' or sentences: 'Joe made tea. And later he cleaned up as well.'

Conjunctions can:
- add one thing to another:
I like rain and I like snow.
- oppose one thing against another:
I like rain but my friend hates it.
- show how one thing is caused by another:
I like snow because it looks great.
- show how one thing is linked to the time of another:
We put on warm clothes then we went out in the snow.

Ways of teaching
At this stage in their language development, children's learning about conjunctions will primarily involve understanding the job conjunctions do with a view towards using a variety in creating their own extended sentences.

About the activities
Photocopiable: Join the sentences
As they join up the separated sentences in this photocopiable, children will be guided by the conjunction that starts the second half of the sentence.

Photocopiable: Missing words
In choosing the right conjunction children will need to consider the job that should be done in the space within each sentence. This will guide them to choose between, for example, a 'but' and a 'because'.

Photocopiable: Make the connection
The completion of the sentences in this photocopiable is directed by the connective at the end of the opening section. Once they have completed the photocopiable, children could try re-doing one of their completed examples with the conjunction altered (for example 'I could eat you but...', 'I could eat you and...')

Following up
Find examples: Children can find a variety of words that connect one thing to another or show the relationship between one thing and another.

Join the sentences

Can you cut out and repair these broken sentences? Find a second clause to match every first clause.

First clause	Second clause
I opened my umbrella	if you want them to grow.
We went to the library	because it was raining.
You need to water seeds	so I played on the slide.
Someone was on the swings	because the chain is broken.
We waited in the car	or a school dinner?
Joe looked for us	so I can buy a computer game.
I had my breakfast	until my birthday.
I can't wait	before I went to school.
Would you like sandwiches	and Lara went in goal.
First I put on my socks	but it was closed.
We played football	after counting to fifty.
I can't ride my bike	then my shoes.
I have to save my pocket money	if you want to go out to play.
We got dressed	after doing PE.
Tidy the classroom	while Mum went in the shop.

❏ Make a list of the words that join one half of a sentence with the other.

Missing words

❏ Look at the spaces in these sentences. They are all words people said. They are real quotes. Which words from the word box could fit? Write as many words as you think could fit in each space. Say them aloud to check if they sound right.

I had to go home _____ it was bedtime.

We didn't play outside _____ it was raining.

We had our sandwiches _____ we got on the bus.

I like juice _____ my mum likes tea.

We put water in the freezer _____ it turned into ice.

You can have a biscuit _____ a cake.

I have got a bike _____ it isn't working.

I haven't seen my friend _____ he moved house.

however	but	
		although
because	while	so
though	when	as
or	after	
before	until	if

❏ Try writing your own sentences using some of these conjunctions.

Make the connection

Can you finish these sentences? Fill in words you think the characters might say.

I'm missing playtime because...

I told you to write a story but...

My old bike broke, however...

I like doing daring things although...

I can sneak out when...

You can go out to play after...

I could eat you or...

I'll cast a spell on you if...

❑ List the words that connect the first part of each sentence to your added words.

Time words

Objective
Investigate how words and phrases signal time

Language issues
Prepositions are words that indicate the link between things. For example, words like 'on' and 'beside' function as prepositions to say where one thing is in relation to another:

vase on the table
vase beside the table.

One particular group of prepositions shows how things are linked in time:

We played before eating
We played after eating
We played while eating.

It is a form of positioning, only in this case the prepositions indicate relative positions in time rather than space.

Ways of teaching
As with conjunctions, this unit develops the understanding and use of a particular set of words and, in doing so, expands children's vocabulary. In such learning, children need to be given chances to think of examples of the type of word concerned and see where they could be used.

About the activities
Photocopiable: Sequence
To rebuild the instructions for the yoghurt pot telephone, children will need to look at the temporal prepositions used at the start of the various sentences.

Photocopiable: The tortoise and the hare
The story of the tortoise and the hare has already been used in Unit 4 of Term 3a. Children may want to use the script there to familiarize themselves with the story and dialogue before using this page to recount the tale.

Photocopiable: Recounted story
The boxes with the temporal prepositions can be used in various ways. Children could cut out all the boxes and:
❑ aim to use at least four in creating a story
❑ aim to use three selected by the teacher in a particular order
❑ a group of five can take one each and create a group story.

Following up
Time word telling: Time words (such as the ones used on photocopiable page 'Recounted story') can be written on cards and placed, face downwards, in the middle of a group of six children. The group then have the task of telling a story, sentence by sentence. One of them starts with an opening. The next one follows on, but first he or she must select one of the cards and then use the selected word as the starter for the sentence. This can send the story forwards, backwards, all over the place!

Preposition questions: Children can quiz a child or an adult about the events of a previous day and try coming up with as many questions containing various temporal prepositions as they can think of, such as, 'What did you do after breakfast?', 'What were you reading while you sat in the classroom?'

Sequence

These instructions for making a 'yoghurt pot telephone' are jumbled up.
❏ Cut out the boxes. Try putting the instructions back in sequence.

Then you thread one end of the string through one of the holes.

While one of you is speaking the other listens at the other end.

First you make a hole in the bottom of each yoghurt pot.

Meanwhile your partner does the same with the other yoghurt pot.

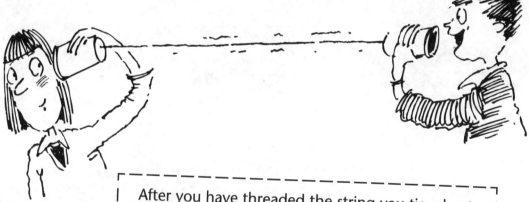

After you have threaded the string you tie a knot.

Once you have threaded string through both ends you stand apart.

When you are far enough from each other for the string to be slightly stretched one of you speaks into your yoghurt pot.

The tortoise and the hare

Can you write the story using the opening words below?

Once... _____

So... _____

Then... _____

When... _____

Later... _____

So... _____

Meanwhile... _____

After... _____

Then... _____

In the end _____

Recounted story

See 'About the activities' on page 140.

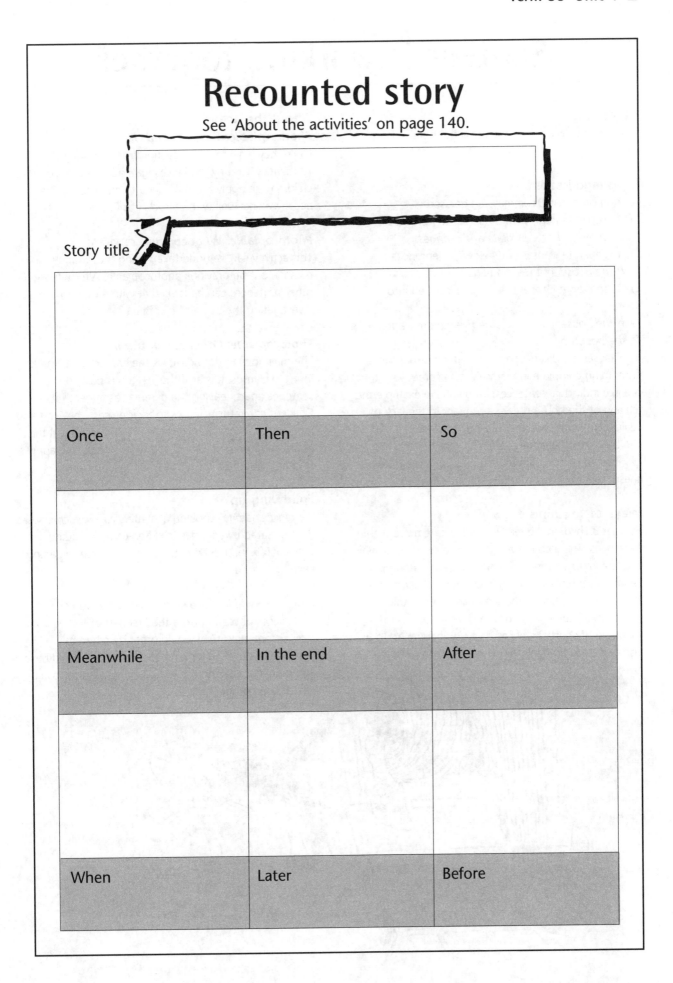

Story title

Once	Then	So
Meanwhile	In the end	After
When	Later	Before

Sentences working together

Objective
Use commas to mark grammatical boundaries in sentences

Language issues
Among other uses, commas can be used
❏ to separate items in a list (see Term 1b Unit 2):
I like coffee, cakes, chocolate and oranges.
❏ to separate clauses (see below) in sentences:
I left the house, not realizing I had no shoes on.
❏ to mark out clauses (see below) inserted into sentences:
I left the house, planning to be five minutes, and walked to the bus stop.

Clauses are distinct parts of sentences that say something complete in themselves. In some ways they are like individual sentences. In the above example the leaving of the house is a separate fact to the lack of realization I was shoeless. Similarly the inserted part of the third example states, separately to the rest, that I planned to be five minutes. Commas can separate off these clauses.

Ways of teaching
By Year 3 children are ready to demarcate more within sentences. There comes a stage in their writing at which the stream of words they produce needs putting into separate sentences. Once this target is achieved there is then a need to extend the sentences from within, otherwise children end up with staccato pieces of writing made up of short sentences. Through beginning to use commas children begin to demarcate within sentences.

About the activities
Photocopiable: Commas and clauses
Once they have read this section from Anthony Horowitz's 'Granny' and investigated the use of commas, children can apply the same idea to other texts. The activity works well with extracts from novels.

Photocopiable: What commas separate
This activity can be undertaken using the 'Granny' passage on the previous photocopiable. Alternatively, other sentences can be looked at with a view towards investigating the use of the comma.

Photocopiable: Commas slot bits in
The main idea in this activity is the way commas mark inserted clauses. It is as if the insert has pushed the sentence apart, leaving the commas as fingerprints. Children can return clauses to their places. They can also look at how the sentence can make sense without the inserted clause. They could see whether this rule applies to other sentences they find with inserted clauses.

Following up
Sentence shading: Looking at sentences in which clauses are separated by commas, children can try shading over the separate clauses to highlight the different meanings each one carries.

Reviewing writing: Following this unit children can re-read pieces of writing from the first part of this year and look at sentences they would organize differently. Specifically, they can look for sentences that could have had more complexity to them and in which they could have placed other clauses.

Commas and clauses

Commas can separate different parts of a sentence.
In each of these sentences from a story two things are being said in one sentence. These are two clauses.
❑ Read each sentence and look at the way the comma separates the two clauses.

Briefly, he scanned the food that lay before him.

There it was, the same as always.

First, there were egg mayonnaise sandwiches, but the eggs had been left out so long that the yellows had taken on a greenish tint.

Granny's home made cakes were dry and heavy, guaranteed to glue the top of your mouth to the bottom of your mouth with little taste in between.

She put the serviettes down and picked up a green porcelain bowl, filled to the brim with thick cream cheese.

Finally she slid the whole thing towards him and as she did so Joe saw the trembling half-smile on her lips, the rattlesnake eyes that pinned him to his seat.

He looked at the cream cheese, slooping about in the bowl with the herring lying there like a dead slug.

Anthony Horowitz: 'Granny'

What commas separate

❏ Look for some sentences with commas. Write **five** in these boxes.

> Briefly, he scanned the food that lay before him.

>

>

>

>

What was the bit before the comma about?

How quickly he did it.

_____

_____

_____

_____

What was the bit after the comma about?

What he did. Looking at food.

_____

_____

_____

_____

Commas slot bits in

Sometimes we slot bits into sentences. Commas mark out the bits slotted in.

> *Finally I found the shop.*

> *Finally, after looking for hours, I found the shop.*

❑ Cut these sentences between the commas and find the clause in the box that slots into the space you have made.

> If you want,   , you can watch some telly.

> The mug,   , fell off the table.

> Joe yelled,   , "Catch me!"

> Do not,   , stroke the dog.

> I typed my story,   , on the computer.

> I found,   , the keys I lost last week.

> My Gran,   , cycled to see me.

> I find,   , my teeth are falling out.

after searching for days

with Sam's help

which was full of juice

as I get older

for any reason

who lives miles away

after tea

as he jumped off the wall

Subject knowledge

1: Preliminary notes about grammar

Grammar involves the way in which words of different types are combined into sentences. The explanatory sections that follow will include definitions of types of word along with notes on how they are combined into sentences.

Three preliminary points about grammar:

❑ Function is all-important. Where a word is placed in relation to another word is crucial in deciding whether it is functioning as a verb or a noun. For example, the word 'run' will often be thought of as a verb. However, in a sentence like 'They went for a run', the word functions as a noun and the verb is 'went'.

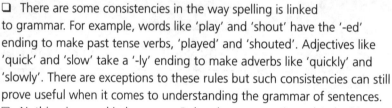

❑ There are some consistencies in the way spelling is linked to grammar. For example, words like 'play' and 'shout' have the '-ed' ending to make past tense verbs, 'played' and 'shouted'. Adjectives like 'quick' and 'slow' take a '-ly' ending to make adverbs like 'quickly' and 'slowly'. There are exceptions to these rules but such consistencies can still prove useful when it comes to understanding the grammar of sentences.

❑ Nothing is sacred in language. Rules change over time, the double negative has gained currency and regional variation in accent and dialect is now far more valued than has been the case in the past. The rules of grammar that follow are subject to change as the language we use lives and grows.

2: Words and functions

Grammar picks out the functions of words. The major classes or types of word in the English language are:

noun

The name of something or someone, including concrete things, such as 'dog' or 'tree', and abstract things, such as 'happiness' or 'fear'.

pronoun

A word that replaces a noun. The noun 'John' in 'John is ill' can be replaced by a pronoun 'he', making 'He is ill'.

verb

A word that denotes an action or a happening. In the sentence 'I ate the cake' the verb is 'ate'. These are sometimes referred to as 'doing' words.

adjective

A word that modifies a noun. In the phrase 'the little boat' the adjective 'little' describes the noun 'boat'.

adverb
A word that modifies a verb. In the phrase 'he slowly walked' the adverb is 'slowly'.

preposition
A word or phrase that shows the relationship of one thing to another. In the phrase 'the house beside the sea' the preposition 'beside' places the two nouns in relation to each other.

conjunction
A word or phrase that joins other words and phrases. A simple example is the word 'and' that joins nouns in 'Snow White and Doc and Sneezy'.

article
The indefinite articles in English are 'a' and 'an' and the definite article is 'the'. Articles appear before nouns and denote whether the noun is specific ('give me the book') or not ('give me a book').

interjection
A word or phrase expressing or exclaiming an emotion, such as 'Oh!' and 'Aaargh!'

The various word types can be found in the following example sentences:

Lou	saw	his	new	house	from	the	train.
noun	verb	pronoun	adjective	noun	preposition	article	noun
Yeow!	I	hit	my	head	on	the	door.
interjection	pronoun	verb	pronoun	noun	preposition	article	noun
Amir	sadly	lost	his	bus fare	down	the	drain.
noun	adverb	verb	pronoun	noun	preposition	article	noun
Give	Jan	a	good	book	for	her	birthday.
verb	noun	article	adjective	noun	conjunction	pronoun	noun

The pages that follow provide more information on these word classes.

Nouns

There are four types of noun in English.
Common nouns are general names for things. For example, in the sentence 'I fed the dog', the noun 'dog' could be used to refer to any dog, not to a specific one. Other examples include 'boy', 'country', 'book', 'apple'.
Proper nouns are the specific names given to identify things or people. In a phrase like 'Sam is my dog' the word 'dog' is the common noun but 'Sam' is a proper noun because it refers to and identifies a specific dog. Other examples include 'the Prime Minister', 'Wales' and 'Amazing Grace'.
Collective nouns refer to a group of things together, such as 'a flock (of sheep)' or 'a bunch (of bananas)'.

A **noun** is the name of someone or something.

Abstract nouns refer to things that are not concrete, such as an action, a concept, an event, quality or state. Abstract nouns like 'happiness' and 'fulfilment' refer to ideas or feelings which are uncountable; others, such as 'hour', 'joke' and 'quantity' are countable.

Nouns can be singular or plural. To change a singular to a plural the usual rule is to add 's'. This table includes other rules to bear in mind, however:

If the singular ends in:	Rule	Examples
'y' after a consonant	Remove 'y', add 'ies'	party → parties
'y' after a vowel	add 's'	donkey → donkeys
'o' after a consonant	add 'es'	potato → potatoes
'o' after a vowel	add 's'	video → videos
a sound like 's', such as 's', 'sh', 'tch', 'x', 'z'	add 'es'	kiss → kisses dish → dishes
		watch → watches
'ch' sounding like it does at the end of 'perch'	add 'es'	church → churches

Pronouns

A **pronoun** is a word that stands in for a noun.

There are different classes of pronoun. The main types are:

Personal pronouns, referring to people or things, such as 'I', 'you', 'it'. The personal pronouns distinguish between subject and object case (I/me, he/him, she/her, we/us, they/them and the archaic thou/thee).

Reflexive pronouns, referring to people or things that are also the subject of the sentence. In the sentence 'You can do this yourself' the pronoun 'yourself' refers to 'you'. Such pronouns end with '-self' or '-selves'. Other examples include 'myself', 'themselves'.

Possessive pronouns identify people or things as belonging to a person or thing. For example, in the sentence 'The book is hers' the possessive pronoun 'hers' refers to 'the book'. Other examples include 'its' and 'yours'. Note that possessive pronouns never take an apostrophe.

Relative pronouns link relative clauses to their nouns. In the sentence 'The man who was in disguise sneaked into the room' the relative clause 'who was in disguise' provides extra information about 'the man'. This relative clause is linked by the relative pronoun 'who'. Other examples include 'whom', 'which' and 'that'.

Interrogative pronouns are used in questions. They refer to the thing that is being asked about. In the question 'What is your name?' and 'Where is the book?' the pronouns 'what' and 'where' stand for the answers – the name and the location of the book.

Demonstrative pronouns are pronouns that 'point'. They are used to show the relation of the speaker to an object. There are four demonstrative pronouns in English: 'this', 'that', 'these', 'those', used as in 'This is my house' and 'That is your house'. They have specific uses, depending upon the position of the object to the speaker:

	Near to speaker	**Far away from speaker**
Singular	this	that
Plural	these	those

Indefinite pronouns stand in for an indefinite noun. The indefinite element can be the number of elements or the nature of them but they are summed up in ambiguous pronouns such as 'any', 'some' or 'several'. Other examples are the pronouns that end with '-body', '-one' and '-thing', such as 'somebody', 'everyone' and 'anything'.

Person
Personal, reflexive and possessive pronouns can be in the first, second or third person.
First person pronouns (I, we) involve the speaker or writer.
Second person pronouns (you) refer to the listener or reader.
Third person pronouns refer to something other than these two participants in the communication (he, she, it, they).
The person of the pronoun will agree with particular forms of verbs: I like/ She likes.

Verbs
The **tense** of a verb places a happening in time. The main three tenses are the present, past and future.

A **verb** is a word that denotes an action or a happening.

To express an action that will take place in the future, verbs appear with 'will' or 'shall' (or 'going to'). The regular past tense is formed by the addition of the suffix '-ed', although some of the most common verbs in English (the 'strong' verbs) have irregular past tenses.

Present tense (happening now)	**Past tense (happened in past)**	**Future tense (to happen in future)**
am, say, find, kick	was, said, found, kicked	will be, will say, shall find, shall kick

Continuous verbs
The present participle form of a verb is used to show a continuous action. Whereas a past tense like 'kicked' denotes an action that happened ('I kicked'), the present participle denotes the action as happening and continuing as it is described ('I was kicking', the imperfect tense, or 'I am kicking', the present continuous). There is a sense in these uses of an action that has not ended.

The present participle usually ends in '-ing', such as 'walking', 'finding', and continuous verbs are made with a form of the verb 'be', such as 'was' or 'am': 'I was running' and 'I am running'.

Auxiliary verbs

Auxiliary verbs 'help' other verbs – they regularly accompany full verbs, always preceding them in a verb phrase. The auxiliary verbs in English can be divided into three categories:

Primary verbs are used to indicate the timing of a verb, such as 'be', 'have' or 'did' (including all their variations such as 'was', 'were', 'has', 'had' and so on). These can be seen at work in verb forms like 'I was watching a film', 'He has finished eating', 'I didn't lose my keys'.

Modal verbs indicate the possibility of an action occurring or the necessity of it happening, such as 'I might watch a film', 'I should finish eating' and 'I shouldn't lose my keys'. The modal verbs in English are: would, could, might, should, can, will, shall, may, and must. These verbs never function on their own as main verbs. They always act as auxiliaries helping other verbs.

Marginal modals, namely 'dare', 'need', 'ought to' and 'used to'. These act as modals, such as in the sentences 'I dared enter the room', 'You need to go away' and 'I ought to eat my dinner', but they can also act as main verbs, as in 'I need cake'.

Adjectives

An **adjective** is a word that modifies a noun.

The main function of adjectives is to define quality or quantity. Examples of the use of descriptions of quality include: 'good story', 'sad day' and 'stupid dog'. Examples of the use of descriptions of quantity include 'some stories', 'ten days' and 'many dogs'.

Adjectives can appear in one of three different degrees of intensity. In the table below it can be seen that there are '-er' and '-est' endings that show an adjective is comparative or superlative, though, as can be seen, there are exceptions. The regular comparative is formed by the addition of the suffix '-er' to shorter words and 'more' to longer words (kind/kinder, beautiful/more beautiful). The regular superlative is formed by the addition of the suffix '-est' to shorter words and 'most' to longer words. Note, however, that some common adjectives have irregular comparatives and superlatives.

Nominative The nominative is the plain form that describes a noun.	**Comparative** The comparative implies a comparison between the noun and something else.	**Superlative** The superlative is the ultimate degree of a particular quality.
Examples	**Examples**	**Examples**
long	longer	longest
small	smaller	smallest
big	bigger	biggest
fast	faster	fastest
bad	worse	worst
good	better	best
far	farther/further	farthest/furthest

Adverbs

Adverbs provide extra information about the time, place or manner in which a verb happened.

| Manner
Provides information about the manner in which the action was done. | Ali *quickly* ran home.
The cat climbed *fearfully* up the tree. |
| --- | --- |
| Time
Provides information about the time at which the action occurred. | *Yesterday* Ali ran home.
Sometimes the cat climbed up the tree. |
| Place
Provides information about where the action took place. | *Outside* Ali ran home.
In the garden the cat climbed up the tree. |

An **adverb** is a word that modifies a verb.

Variations in the degree of intensity of an adverb are indicated by other adjectives such as 'very', 'rather', 'quite' and 'somewhat'. Comparative forms include 'very quickly', 'rather slowly', and 'most happily'.

The majority of single-word adverbs are made by adding '-ly' to an adjective: 'quick/quickly', 'slow/slowly' and so on.

Prepositions

Prepositions show how nouns or pronouns are positioned in relation to other nouns and pronouns in the same sentence. This can often be the location of one thing in relation to another in space, such as 'on', 'over', 'near'; or time, such as 'before', 'after'.

Prepositions are usually placed before a noun. They can consist of one word ('The cat *in* the tree...'), two words ('The cat *close to* the gate...') or three ('The cat *on top of* the roof...').

A **preposition** is a word or phrase that shows the relationship of one thing to another.

Conjunctions

Conjunctions can join words or clauses in one of four ways:

Name of conjunction	Nature of conjunction	Examples
Addition	One or more things together	We had our tea *and* went out to play. It was a cold day – *also* it rained.
Opposition	One or more things in opposition	I like coffee *but* my brother hates it. It could rain *or* it could snow.
Time	One or more things connected over time	Toby had his tea *then* went out to play. The bus left *before* we reached the stop.
Cause	One or more things causing or caused by another	I took a map *so that* we wouldn't get lost. We got lost *because* we had the wrong map.

A **conjunction** is a word or phrase that joins other words and phrases.

3: Understanding sentences

Types of sentence

The four main types of sentence are **declarative**, **interrogative**, **imperative** and **exclamatory**. The function of a sentence has an effect on the word order; imperatives, for example, often begin with a verb.

Sentence type	Function	Examples
Declarative	Makes a statement	The house is down the lane. Joe rode the bike.
Interrogative	Asks a question	Where is the house? What is Joe doing?
Imperative	Issues a command or direction	Turn left at the traffic lights. Get on your bike!
Exclamatory	Issues an interjection	Wow, what a mess! Oh no!

Sentences: Clauses and complexities

Phrases

A phrase is a set of words performing a grammatical function. In the sentence 'The little, old, fierce dog brutally chased the sad and fearful cat', there are three distinct units performing grammatical functions. The first phrase in this sentence essentially names the dog and provides descriptive information. This is a noun phrase, performing the job of a noun – 'the little, old, fierce dog'. To do this the phrase uses adjectives. The important thing to look out for is the way in which words build around a key word in a phrase. So here the words 'little', 'old' and 'fierce' are built around the word 'dog'. In examples like these, 'dog' is referred to as the **headword** and the adjectives are termed **modifiers**. Together, the modifier and headword make up the noun phrase. Modifiers can also come after the noun, as in 'The little, old, fierce dog that didn't like cats brutally chased the sad and fearful cat'. In this example 'little, 'old' and 'fierce' are **premodifiers** and the phrase 'that didn't like cats' is a **postmodifier**.

The noun phrase is just one of the types of phrase that can be made.

Phrase type	Examples
Noun phrase	The *little, old fierce dog* didn't like cats. She gave him *a carefully and colourfully covered book*.
Verb phrase	The dog *had been hiding* in the house. The man *climbed through* the window without a sound.
Adjectival phrase	The floor was *completely clean*. The floor was *so clean you could eat your dinner off it*.
Adverbial phrase	I finished my lunch *very slowly indeed*. *More confidently than usual*, she entered the room.
Prepositional phrase	The cat sat *at the top of* the tree. The phone rang *in the middle of* the night.

Notice that phrases can appear within phrases. A noun phrase like 'carefully and colourfully covered book' contains the adjectival phrase 'carefully and colourfully covered'. This string of words forms the adjectival phrase in which the words 'carefully' and 'colourfully' modify the adjective 'covered'. Together these words 'carefully and colourfully covered' modify the noun 'book', creating a distinct noun phrase. This is worth noting as it shows how the boundaries between phrases can be blurred, a fact that can cause confusion unless borne in mind!

Clauses

Clauses are units of meaning included within a sentence, usually containing a verb and other elements linked to it. 'The burglar ran' is a clause containing the definite article, noun and verb; 'The burglar quickly ran from the little house' is also a clause that adds an adverb, preposition and adjective. The essential element in a clause is the verb. Clauses look very much like small sentences, indeed sentences can be constructed of just one clause: 'The burglar hid', 'I like cake'.

Sentences can also be constructed out of a number of clauses linked together: 'The burglar ran and I chased him because he stole my cake.' This sentence contains three clauses: 'The burglar ran', 'I chased him', 'he stole my cake'.

Clauses and phrases: the difference

Clauses include participants in an action denoted by a verb. Phrases, however, need not necessarily contain a verb. These phrases make little sense on their own: 'without a sound', 'very slowly indeed'. They work as part of a clause.

Simple, compound and complex sentences

The addition of clauses can make complex or compound sentences.

Simple sentences are made up of one clause, for example: 'The dog barked', 'Sam was scared'.

Compound sentences are made up of clauses added to clauses. In compound sentences each of the clauses is of equal value; no clause is dependent on another. An example of a compound sentence is: 'The dog barked and the parrot squawked'. Both these clauses are of equal importance: 'The dog barked', 'the parrot squawked'.

Other compound sentences include, for example: 'I like coffee and I like chocolate', 'I like coffee, but I don't like tea'.

Complex sentences are made up of a main clause with a subordinate clause or clauses. Subordinate clauses make sense in relation to the main clause. They say something about it and are dependent upon it, for example in the sentences: 'The dog barked because he saw a burglar', 'Sam was scared so he phoned the police'.

In both these cases the subordinate clause ('he saw a burglar', 'he phoned the police') is elaborating on the main clause. They explain why the dog barked or why Sam was scared and, in doing so, are subordinate to those actions. The reader needs to see the main clauses to fully appreciate what the subordinate ones are stating.

Subject and object

The **subject** of a sentence or clause is the agent that performs the action denoted by the verb – '*Shaun* threw the ball'. The **object** is the agent to which the verb is done – 'ball'. It could be said that the subject does the verb to the object (a simplification but a useful one). The simplest type of sentence is known as the SVO (subject–verb–object) sentence (or clause), as in 'You lost your way', 'I found the book' and 'Lewis met Chloe'.

The active voice and the passive voice

These contrast two ways of saying the same thing:

Active voice	Passive voice
I found the book.	The book was found by me.
Megan met Ben.	Ben was met by Megan.
The cow jumped over the moon.	The moon was jumped over by the cow.

The two types of clause put the same subject matter in a different **voice**. Passive clauses are made up of a subject and verb followed by an agent.

The book	was found by	me.
subject	verb	agent
Ben	was met by	Megan.
subject	verb	agent

Sentences can be written in the active or the passive voice. A sentence can be changed from the active to the passive voice by:
❑ moving the subject to the end of the clause
❑ moving the object to the start of the clause
❑ changing the verb or verb phrase by placing a form of the verb 'be' before it (as in 'was found')
❑ changing the verb or verb phrase by placing 'by' after it.

In passive clauses the agent can be deleted, either because it does not need mentioning or because a positive choice is made to omit it. Texts on science may leave out the agent, with sentences such as 'The water is added to the salt and stirred'.

4: Punctuation

Punctuation provides marks within sentences that guide the reader. Speech doesn't need punctuation (and would sound bizarre if it included noises for full stops etc). In speech, much is communicated by pausing, changing tone and so on. In writing, the marks within and around a sentence provide indications of when to pause, when something is being quoted and so on.

Punctuation mark	Uses	Examples
A	**Capital letter** 1. Start a sentence. 2. Indicate proper nouns. 3. Emphasize certain words.	All I want is cake. You can call me Al. I want it TOMORROW!
.	**Full stop** Ends sentences that are not questions or exclamations.	This is a sentence.
?	**Question mark** Ends a sentence that is a question.	Is this a question?
!	**Exclamation mark** Ends a sentence that is an exclamation.	Don't do that!
" " ' '	**Quotation (speech) marks (or inverted commas)** Enclose direct speech. Can be double or single.	"Help me," the man yelled. 'Help me,' the man yelled.
,	**Comma** 1. Places a pause between clauses within a sentence. 2. Separates items in a list. 3. Separates adjectives in a series. 4. Completely encloses clauses inserted in a sentence. 5. Marks speech from words denoting who said them.	We were late, although it didn't matter. You will need eggs, butter, salt and flour. I wore a long, green, frilly skirt. We were, after we had rushed to get there, late for the film. 'Thank you,' I said.
—	**Hyphen** Connects elements of certain words.	Co-ordinator, south-west.
:	**Colon** 1. Introduces lists (including examples).	To go skiing these are the main items you will need: a hat, gloves, goggles and sunscreen.

continued...

Punctuation mark	Uses	Examples
	2. Introduces summaries. 3. Introduces (direct) quotations. 4. Introduces a second clause that expands or illustrates the meaning of the first.	We have learned the following on the ski slope: do a snow plough to slow down… My instructor always says: 'Bend those knees.' The snow hardened: it turned into ice.
;	**Semicolon** 1. Separates two closely linked clauses, and shows there is a link between them. 2. Separates items in a complex list.	On Tuesday, the bus was late; the train was early. You can go by aeroplane, train and taxi; Channel tunnel train, coach, then a short walk; or aeroplane and car.
'	**Apostrophe of possession** Denotes the ownership of one thing by another (see page 160).	This is Mona's scarf. These are the teachers' books.
'	**Apostrophe of contraction** Shows the omission of a letter(s) when two (or occasionally more) words are contracted.	Don't walk on the grass.
•••	**Ellipsis** 1. Shows the omission of words. 2. Indicates a pause.	The teacher moaned, 'Look at this floor… a mess… this class…' Lou said: 'I think I locked the door… no, hang on, did I?'
( )	**Brackets** Contains a parenthesis – a word or phrase added to a sentence to give a bit more information.	The cupboard (which had been in my family for years) was broken.
—	**Dash** 1. Indicates additional information, with more emphasis than a comma. 2. Indicates a pause, especially for effect at the end of a sentence. 3. Contains extra information (used instead of brackets).	She is a teacher – and a very good one too. We all know what to expect – the worst. You finished that job – and I don't know how – before the deadline.

Adding an apostrophe of possession

The addition of an apostrophe can create confusion. The main thing to look at is the noun – ask:

❏ Is it singular or plural?
❏ Does it end in an 's'?

If the noun is singular and doesn't end in 's', you add an apostrophe and an 's', for example: Indra's house the firefighter's bravery	If the noun is singular and ends in 's', you add an apostrophe and an 's', for example: the bus's wheels Thomas's pen
If the noun is plural and doesn't end in 's', you add an apostrophe and an 's', for example: the women's magazine the geese's flight	If the noun is plural and ends in 's', you add an apostrophe but don't add an 's', for example: the boys' clothes the dancers' performance

Further reading

Carter, R; Goddard, A; Reah, D; Sanger, K; Bowring, K (1997) *Working with Texts: A Core Book for Language Analysis*, Routledge

Crystal, D (1988) *Rediscover Grammar with David Crystal*, Longman

Crystal, D (1995) *The Cambridge Encyclopedia of the English Language*, Cambridge University Press
A big volume but very accessible, covering many areas of English including grammar, punctuation and dialect. Filled with interesting asides and examples from sources as varied as Shakespeare to Monty Python.

Hurford, R (1994) *Grammar: A student's guide*, Cambridge University Press
An excellent text, setting out basic guidelines on the workings of grammar.

Reah, D and Ross, A (1997) *Exploring Grammar: Main Routes and Scenic Paths*, WordsWork
A popular and accessible introductory course to grammar with interesting exercises to guide the reader.

Sealey, A (1996) *Learning About Language: Issues for Primary Teachers*, Open University Press
A more theoretical work that presents some of the issues and arguments surrounding knowledge about language.